I0098650

WHAT'S NEXT?
PREPARING FOR THE RAPTURE

JIMMY EVANS
MARK HITCHCOCK

WHAT'S NEXT?
PREPARING FOR THE RAPTURE

JIMMY EVANS
MARK HITCHCOCK

TIPPING POINT
— PRESS —

TIPPING POINT
— P R E S S —

What's Next? Preparing for the Rapture
Copyright © 2024 by Jimmy Evans and Mark Hitchcock

Scripture quotations are from the ESV® Bible (The Holy Bible, English
Standard Version®), © 2001 by Crossway, a publishing ministry of Good
News Publishers. Used by permission. All rights reserved. The ESV text
may not be quoted in any publication made available to the public by a
Creative Commons license. The ESV may not be translated in whole or in
part into any other language.

All rights reserved. No portion of this publication may be reproduced,
stored in a retrieval system, or transmitted in any form by any means—
electronic, mechanical, photocopying, recording, or any other—without
prior permission from the publisher.

ISBN: 978-1-960870-39-1 Paperback
ISBN: 978-1-960870-40-7 eBook
ISBN: 979-8-89153-524-4 Audiobook

Tipping Point Press creates resources to help people understand biblical
prophecy and the relevance of world events to the End Times. These
messages provide hope, peace, and encouragement. For more resources
visit EndTimes.com.

Tipping Point Press
1021 Grace Lane
Southlake, TX 76092

While the authors make every effort to provide accurate URLs at the time
of printing for external or third-party internet websites, neither they nor
the publisher assume any responsibility for changes or errors made after
publication.

Printed in the United States of America

24 25 26 27—5 4 3 2 1

Contents

Introduction

Why Is the Rapture Important?

As ministers of the gospel and students of Bible prophecy, we firmly believe that the Rapture of the Church is the next major event on God's prophetic calendar. All around us, we see the signs that the Bible predicted converging and intensifying, signifying Christ's return is very close. These signs are like birth pains before the delivery of a new baby. Geopolitical instability, moral decay, apostasy in the Church, the rise of globalism, Israel's rebirth as a nation, and many other indicators point to the soon return of Jesus. It's as if God is shouting from the heavens, "The King is coming! Get up and get ready!"

The Doctrine of Imminency

The Bible teaches that the Rapture is *imminent,* which means it could happen at any moment with no new signs or events that must precede it. Jesus urged His followers to be watchful and ready for His return (Matthew 24:42, 44; 25:13). The apostles wrote as if Christ could come in their lifetime

(1 Thessalonians 1:10; James 5:7–9). For 2,000 years, the Church has been living with the constant expectation of His appearing (Titus 2:13). And today, that Blessed Hope burns brighter than ever as we see the Day approaching (Hebrews 10:25).

Why Do We Need to Understand the Rapture?

In a world that is growing darker, the promise of the Rapture shines as a beacon of hope for believers. It is God's ultimate deliverance that we eagerly anticipate (1 Corinthians 1:7; Philippians 3:20). As Christ's bride, we should be longing for that moment when our Bridegroom will come and take us to the Father's House (John 14:2–3). But more than just a comforting doctrine, believing and understanding the Rapture are powerful motivators for how we should live and minister in these last days.

Since Jesus could come at any second, we need to be serious, alert, and focused on eternal priorities (1 Peter 4:7). The Rapture should encourage us to live godly lives as we prepare to meet our King (2 Peter 3:11–12). It should shape our values, goals, and lifestyle choices. Like the wise virgins in Jesus' parable, we need to be ready with oil in our lamps, which means we should invest our time and talents for God's glory until Jesus comes to take us to the Father's House (Matthew 25:1–13).

The Rapture should also create an urgency in our witness and a passion to reach lost people with the

Good News. When Jesus returns, those left behind will face the horrors of the Tribulation, the most terrible time in human history (Matthew 24:21). We may not have another chance to tell our unsaved friends and loved ones about Jesus. Like the apostle Paul, we should be willing to do all things for the sake of the gospel (1 Corinthians 9:22–23).

The Rapture is meant to be a source of comfort and encouragement during difficult times (1 Thessalonians 4:18). No matter what we face in this life, we know our ultimate hope is secure in Heaven (1 Peter 1:3–6).

> For I consider that the sufferings of this present time are not worth comparing with the glory that is to be revealed to us (Romans 8:18).

> When Christ who is your life appears, then you also will appear with him in glory (Colossians 3:4).

Understanding the truth of the Rapture gives us an eternal perspective that keeps us anchored through life's storms.

Yet the doctrine of the Rapture has fallen on hard times recently. Many Christians, even from Bible-believing churches, have only a vague understanding of it. Some prominent leaders question or outright deny the Rapture, especially the pre-Tribulation timing of it. And the world mocks and scoffs at the idea of Christ's imminent return (2 Peter 3:3–4).

We saw this ridicule and derision most recently during the total eclipse over the US on April 8, 2024. Many people on social media found humor in being marked "safe" from the Rapture. There were hundreds of jokes and memes. Sadly, many people passing around those jokes were conservative Christians. First, we don't know of a single reputable end-times Bible teacher who thought the eclipse would coincide with the Rapture. Second, Jesus did tell us to watch the signs in the heavens (Luke 21:25–26). It only makes sense that the devil would use such a remarkable event to make people doubt the return of the Lord.

Our Purpose and Goals

That's why we wrote this book. As much as we love teaching about the Rapture, our hearts are heavy that so many are unclear or deceived regarding it. The Church and world need a clear, authoritative, and engaging treatment of this vital biblical truth now more than ever.

Our goals are to equip you with:

- A comprehensive understanding of the Rapture, its importance, and how it relates to end-times events

- Biblical answers to the most common questions and objections about the Rapture

- A deeper awareness of the signs indicating the Rapture is at hand

- An eternal perspective that shapes your priorities and produces a joy-filled expectancy for Christ's return

- A greater passion to share the gospel with the lost in light of the coming Tribulation

- An exhortation to faithfully occupy and invest your life for God's glory until Jesus comes

There has never been a more crucial time for believers to be grounded in what the Bible teaches about things to come. The Rapture is not just an academic issue for prophecy buffs or a fantasy for those obsessed with escaping reality. It is the joyful anticipation and confident assurance of the Church, based on God's unchanging Word.

Why Is This Book Unique?

While there are many helpful books on the Rapture and End Times, we believe this one offers a unique combination of:

- A clear, readable, and engaging style that makes complex prophetic concepts easy to grasp

- A comprehensive biblical treatment that integrates key Rapture passages with the overall flow of end-times events

- Answers to the most up-to-date arguments, objections, and alternative views on the Rapture

- Insights from decades of intensive study and ministry experience dedicated to proclaiming the soon return of Christ

It is our earnest prayer that the Lord will use this book to stir your heart with a passion for His appearing, to equip your mind with prophetic truth, and to impact your life with an eternal perspective. As you read these pages, may the Blessed Hope of the Rapture become a living reality that anchors your soul, motivates your service, and fills you with joyful expectation.

What to Expect in the Coming Chapters

As you journey through this book, here's a snapshot of what you'll discover in each chapter:

- **Chapter 1:** Defining the Rapture
  In this foundational chapter, we define the meaning of the term "rapture," explore the key biblical passages that teach it, and show how it is a distinct event from the Second Coming of Christ.

- **Chapter 2:** Answering Rapture Objections
  Here, we tackle head-on the most frequent objections, questions, and misconceptions about the Rapture, providing concise biblical answers to strengthen your understanding and equip you to respond to critics.

- **Chapter 3:** The Timing of the Rapture
  This chapter dives into the various positions on the timing of the Rapture in relation to the Tribulation—pre, mid, pre-wrath, and post. We make a compelling biblical case for the pre-Tribulation view.

- **Chapter 4:** The Bible and the Rapture
  Focusing on the Rapture in both testaments, we trace it through the types and shadows of the Old Testament, the teachings of Jesus, and the epistles of Paul and others to show that it's a major biblical theme.

- **Chapter 5:** General Signs the Rapture Is Near
  In this eye-opening section, we demonstrate that the general signs of the End Times the Bible predicts—apostasy, moral decay, false teaching, and others—are increasing in unprecedented convergence, indicating the Rapture is near.

- **Chapter 6:** Specific Societal and Cultural Signs
  Here, we zero in on how specific developments such as the breakdown of the family, the rise of globalism and one-world government, the move toward a cashless society, and more are setting the stage for the Rapture and Tribulation.

- **Chapter 7:** Developments Involving Israel and the Middle East
  Updating you with the current events, we show how the super sign of Israel's miraculous

rebirth and the growing alignment of nations against her are the key indications that the prophetic clock is ticking towards the Tribulation and Christ's coming.

- **Chapter 8:** Astronomical Signs in the Heavens
  Not even the universe is silent as God signals the last days! We explore the biblical significance of blood moons, solar eclipses, constellations, and other celestial wonders that have captured the world's attention in recent years.

- **Chapter 9:** Meeting Jesus in the Air
  Moving from the prophetic signs to the Rapture event itself, this thrilling chapter walks through the details of that "twinkling of an eye" moment when believers will be transformed, resurrected, and raptured to meet the Lord in the air!

- **Chapter 10:** The Resurrection and Transformation of Believers
  Here, we revel in the amazing realities of the resurrection of the dead in Christ and the transformation of the living that will instantly occur at the Rapture, resulting in new, immortal, and incorruptible bodies conformed to Christ's glory.

- **Chapter 11:** The Judgment Seat of Christ and Marriage Supper of the Lamb
  Shifting the scene to Heaven, this chapter explores the two major events believers will

participate in following the Rapture—the Bema Seat evaluation of our lives and the glorious celebratory Feast of the Lamb and His Bride!

- **Chapter 12:** The Tribulation and the Antichrist
  What will happen on earth after the Rapture? We paint a sobering picture of the unprecedented misery of the Tribulation years, yet also highlight the unprecedented harvest that will take place in the midst of judgment.

- **Chapter 13:** Second Coming, Millennium, and Eternity
  In the final chapter, we follow the culmination of history from Christ's glorious return and defeat of the Antichrist, to Jesus' Millennial Reign, to the final vanquishing of Satan and sin, and finally to the eternal joys of New Heavens and New Earth.

So fasten your seatbelt and prepare for an exhilarating journey through the Bible's prophetic roadmap, with the Rapture at the heart of it all! And may you be found ready and watching when the trumpet sounds and Christ steps from the heavenly scene with the shout "Come up here!"

1

Defining the Rapture

The Origin of the Term

The Rapture of the Church is one of the most exciting and encouraging promises in all of Scripture.
It is the "Blessed Hope" that we as believers are to
eagerly anticipate (Titus 2:13). The term *rapture*
comes from the Latin verb *rapio*,[1] meaning "to
catch up" or "to snatch away." While the actual
word doesn't appear in most English translations,
the concept is clearly taught in Scripture passages
like 1 Thessalonians 4:15–18, which states:

> For this we declare to you by a word from the Lord,
> that we who are alive, who are left until the coming
> of the Lord, will not precede those who have fallen
> asleep. For the Lord himself will descend from heaven
> with a cry of command, with the voice of an archangel,
> and with the sound of the trumpet of God. And the
> dead in Christ will rise first. Then we who are alive,
> who are left, will be caught up together with them
> in the clouds to meet the Lord in the air, and so we
> will always be with the Lord. Therefore encourage one
> another with these words.

The apostle Paul depicts Christ descending from Heaven, resurrecting believers who have died, and then transforming living believers to meet Him in the air. The Greek word used for "caught up" in verse 17 is *harpazo,* which means 'to seize, carry off by force, or snatch away.' The Latin Vulgate translates *harpazo* as *rapiemur,* so there is a strong historical connection between Greek and English via Latin.

The Rapture refers to the future event when Jesus Christ will suddenly descend from Heaven, snatch up His followers (the Church) from the earth, and take them to Heaven to be with Him forever. Those believers who have died will be resurrected and caught up first. Then those believers who are alive on the earth when Christ returns will be transformed and caught up together with the resurrected saints to meet the Lord in the air.

Paul provides additional details about the Rapture in 1 Corinthians 15:51–53:

> Behold! I tell you a mystery. We shall not all sleep, but we shall all be changed, in a moment, in the twinkling of an eye, at the last trumpet. For the trumpet will sound, and the dead will be raised imperishable, and we shall be changed. For this perishable body must put on the imperishable, and this mortal body must put on immortality.

Here we learn that the Rapture will involve an instantaneous transformation of believers. Our mortal, corruptible bodies will be changed into immortal, incorruptible bodies fit for Heaven. This transformation will happen in the blink of an eye, faster than we can imagine.

An Ancient Idea

It's important to understand that the Rapture is not a new or novel idea. We will go into more detail about this subject in the next chapter. However, it has been the consistent hope and expectation of the Church throughout history. Early church fathers like Irenaeus, Hippolytus, and Cyprian wrote about the imminent return of Christ to catch away His saints. The post-Nicene fathers, including John Chrysostom and Jerome, also affirmed the Rapture. Even Augustine, who is often cited as the father of amillennialism, believed in a future Rapture distinct from the Second Coming.

Reformers such as John Calvin and the Westminster divines taught that Christ would come for His saints before the Tribulation period. Prominent pastors and teachers like Charles Spurgeon, Dwight L. Moody, and Harry Ironside proclaimed the precious promise of the Rapture. In short, belief in the Rapture has been a part of orthodox Christianity from the very beginning.

Different from the Second Coming

It is critical for us to distinguish the Rapture from the Return of Christ to establish His Kingdom. While the

Rapture and the Return are often confused, they are actually two separate events. At the Rapture, Jesus comes in the air for His saints (1 Thessalonians 4:16–17). At the Second Coming, He returns to the earth with His saints (Zechariah 14:5; Revelation 19:14). The Rapture will happen in a moment, in the twinkling of an eye (1 Corinthians 15:51–52). The Second Coming will be a gradual, visible event where "every eye will see Him" (Revelation 1:7).

At the Rapture, Christians will be removed from the earth and taken to Heaven (John 14:2–3). At the Second Coming, believers will return with Christ to the earth to enter the Millennial Kingdom (Revelation 19:11–20:6). The Rapture is imminent and could happen at any moment (Titus 2:13). The Second Coming will be preceded by the Tribulation and many signs (Matthew 24:1–30). The Rapture is a message of hope and comfort (1 Thessalonians 4:18). The Second Coming is a message of judgment (Jude 14–15). At the Rapture, Christ comes as our Bridegroom to take us to the Father's House (John 14:2–3). At the Second Coming, Jesus comes as King of kings to execute judgment and set up His Kingdom on earth (Revelation 19:11–16).

Understanding the distinction between the Rapture and the Second Coming is necessary for us to interpret Bible prophecy accurately. The Rapture is the next event on God's prophetic calendar. It could happen at any moment. There are no prophetic events that must occur before the Rapture. But many prophecies must be fulfilled before the

Second Coming. The Rapture is a sign-less event, and by that we mean all the signs have already occurred. The Second Coming will be preceded by numerous signs that still must take place.

The purposes of the Rapture and the Second Coming are also different. The Rapture occurs before the Tribulation period, which is a time of God's judgment on the earth (1 Thessalonians 5:9; Revelation 3:10). At the Rapture, Jesus will deliver believers from the wrath to come. However, at the Second Coming, Jesus will return after the Tribulation to pour out His wrath on the unbelieving world (Revelation 19:11–21). The Rapture involves Jesus coming for His bride, the Church, to take us to Heaven (1 Thessalonians 4:14–17). The Second Coming involves Jesus coming with His bride to set up His Kingdom on earth (Revelation 19:7–9, 14).

To grasp just how different the Rapture and Second Coming are, consider the analogy of a wedding. In Jewish culture, the bridegroom would go to prepare a place for his bride. Once the place was ready, he would return to get his bride and take her to the home he had prepared, usually as part of his father's household. The wedding ceremony would take place privately, followed by a public celebration. In a similar way, at the Rapture, Christ will come like a bridegroom to snatch away His bride, the Church, and take her to the place He has prepared for her in Heaven (John 14:2–3). After the private wedding ceremony, which parallels the Bema Seat Judgment of believers in Heaven, Christ will return with His bride at the

Second Coming to reign on the earth. The public celebration will then commence (Revelation 19:7–9).

This wedding analogy also highlights the imminency of the Rapture. Just as the bride would eagerly await return of the bridegroom at any moment, we as the Church should live in perpetual readiness for Christ's coming. We don't know when He will appear, but we should live as though it could be at any time. That's why the New Testament resounds with exhortations to watch for Christ's return. Jesus told His disciples in Mark 13:35–37,

> "Therefore stay awake—for you do not know when the master of the house will come, in the evening, or at midnight, or when the rooster crows, or in the morning—lest he come suddenly and find you asleep. And what I say to you I say to all: Stay awake."

Paul likewise urged the Romans,

> Besides this you know the time, that the hour has come for you to wake from sleep. For salvation is nearer to us now than when we first believed. The night is far gone; the day is at hand. So then let us cast off the works of darkness and put on the armor of light (Romans 13:11–12).

To the Philippians, Paul declared,

> But our citizenship is in heaven, and from it we await a Savior, the Lord Jesus Christ, who will transform our lowly body to be like his glorious body, by the power

that enables him even to subject all things to himself (Philippians 3:20–21).

And to Titus, he described the Rapture as our "blessed hope" (Titus 2:13).

One of the most comforting promises regarding the Rapture is that it will happen suddenly, in a moment, in the twinkling of an eye (1 Corinthians 15:51–52). In other words, it will be a split-second transformation. Those who are alive when the Rapture occurs will be changed instantly from mortality to immortality. And those believers who have died will be raised in immortal bodies like Christ's glorious resurrection body (Philippians 3:20–21; 1 John 3:2).

To illustrate the imminency and unexpectedness of the Rapture, Jesus used the examples of the days of Noah and Lot (Luke 17:26–30). In those days, people were going about their daily lives, unaware of the impending judgment. Then suddenly, destruction came. In the days of Noah, people were eating, drinking, marrying, and being given in marriage right up until Noah entered the ark and the Great Flood came.

Similarly, in the days of Lot, people in Sodom were carrying on business as usual, indifferent to the coming wrath. Then in one day, God rained down fire and brimstone on them. Jesus said that's how it will be when He returns to rapture His followers. People will be going about their lives, oblivious to the coming judgment. Then suddenly, in a moment, believers will be caught up to meet the Lord, while unbelievers are left behind to face the Tribulation.

When the Rapture occurs, it will be selective. Jesus gave several examples in Luke 17:34–36. Two people will be in one bed; one will be taken and the other left. Two women will be grinding at the mill; one will be taken and the other left. Two men will be in the field; one will be taken and the other left. In other words, when Christ comes, there will be a supernatural, instantaneous selection and separation of believers and unbelievers. In the twinkling of an eye, believers will be snatched up to Heaven, while unbelievers are left behind to face the judgments that will come upon the earth.

The Old Testament provides several vivid pictures and types of the Rapture. These foreshadowings, which we will discuss in more detail in Chapter 4, help us understand the New Testament truth. For example, in Genesis 5, we read about Enoch who "walked with God, and he was not, for God took him" (Genesis 5:24). The writer of Hebrews explains that Enoch did not see death but was taken up by God, as a picture of what will happen to believers who are alive at the Rapture (Hebrews 11:5). We also see types of the Rapture in Isaiah who was caught up to the Throne of God (Isaiah 6) and Elijah who was taken to Heaven in a whirlwind (2 Kings 2).

Jesus Himself spoke of the Rapture on multiple occasions. In Luke 21:36, He told His disciples to watch and pray always that they may be counted worthy to escape the judgment that would come upon the whole earth. On the night before His death, Jesus comforted His disciples with the promise that He would come again and receive them to Himself, that where He is, there they may be also (John 14:1–3). Jesus spoke of His return to catch away His followers as a source of great joy and hope.

Our Blessed Hope

The Rapture is truly the "blessed hope" of the Church (Titus 2:13). It is our joyful expectation and longing. No matter how difficult our trials, we can find hope and comfort in the promise of Christ's imminent return to take us to be with Him. Whether we face financial troubles, health issues, or persecution for our faith, we can look forward to the day when we will see our Savior face-to-face and be delivered from this sin-cursed world.

The Rapture is also our motivation for godly living. Knowing that Jesus could come at any moment, we ought to strive to be pure as He is pure (1 John 3:2–3). We should be ambitious in our desire to please Him in everything we do, because one day very soon, we will stand before Him to give an account of our thoughts and actions (2 Corinthians 5:9–10). The Rapture should make us urgent in our witness, recognizing that soon, unbelievers will be left behind to endure the horrors of the Tribulation (1 Thessalonians 5:3).

Over and over again in the New Testament, we are exhorted to look for and eagerly await our Lord's return. Paul commended the Thessalonians for waiting for God's Son from Heaven, Jesus, who will rescue us from the coming wrath (1 Thessalonians 1:10). The writer of Hebrews promises that Christ will appear a second time to bring salvation to those who eagerly await Him (Hebrews 9:28). James encouraged his readers to be patient and stand firm because the Lord's coming is near (James 5:7–8). Peter assured his audience that Jesus will be revealed in the last time for their sake (1 Peter 1:5, 13). John pointed believers to the hope of becoming like Christ when He appears (1 John 3:2).

Jesus told a parable about servants who were waiting for their master to return from a wedding banquet. He said,

> "Blessed are those servants whom the master finds awake when he comes. Truly, I say to you, he will dress himself for service and have them recline at table, and he will come and serve them" (Luke 12:37).

Then Jesus ended the parable by urging His followers:

> "You also must be ready, for the Son of Man is coming at an hour you do not expect" (Luke 12:40).

No one knows the day or hour of Christ's return (Matthew 24:36). But we are called to anticipate and prepare for it as though it could happen at any moment. As believers, we should live every day in light of the Rapture.

Our Rescue

The Rapture is our rescue from the outpouring of God's wrath during the Tribulation period. Paul assures us,

> For God has not destined us for wrath, but to obtain salvation through our Lord Jesus Christ, (1 Thessalonians 5:9).

Jesus also told the church in Philadelphia,

> "Because you have kept my word about patient endurance, I will keep you from the hour of trial that is coming on the whole world, to try those who dwell on the earth" (Revelation 3:10).

Those who ridicule the promise of the Rapture need to understand that the Church is missing from the earth during the Tribulation judgments described in Revelation chapters 6–18. The redeemed are seen in Heaven around God's Throne, rejoicing and preparing for Christ's Second Coming. But never once are Church-Age believers (believers prior to the Rapture) seen under God's wrath on earth during the Tribulation. The Rapture will deliver the Church from that horrendous time of judgment.

To be clear, the Rapture is not a second chance for salvation before the Tribulation. It is the full manifestation of the salvation that believers in Jesus Christ already possess. Once the Church is removed from the earth and the Antichrist is revealed, those who reject the gospel during the Tribulation will be met with a strong delusion from God who "sends them a strong delusion, so that they may believe what is false" (2 Thessalonians 2:11). For them, it will be too late. They will still have an opportunity to accept the gospel, but they will not be rescued from God's wrath. But for all who are in Christ, the Rapture will be a glorious deliverance. To use an Old Testament foreshadowing, like Noah, we will be safe inside the ark before the flood of God's judgment falls.

No Reason for Fear or Idleness

Yes, the Rapture is our "blessed hope." It's not a spooky concept that should evoke fear or dread in Christians. Instead, it is a promise of reunion with loved ones in Christ who have already died and union with our Savior whom we adore (1 Thessalonians 4:17–18). It is an incentive for us to pursue godliness, knowing that our ultimate redemption is drawing near. It is a rescue operation, not an enemy invasion:

> "Now when these things begin to take place, straighten up and raise your heads, because your redemption is drawing near" (Luke 21:28).

While skeptics and scoffers may argue that Jesus has delayed His coming, God is not slack concerning His promises, which means He is right on time—His time. He is patient. He wants to save many more people. Our only appropriate response is to repent and believe (2 Peter 3:3–9). For the unbeliever, the Rapture will come as an unexpected thief in the night. But for followers of Jesus, the Rapture should be our glorious anticipation.

No, we don't know the day or the hour. But we can know the season. The signs of Christ's return are shouting to us that His coming is near. The Rapture has never been more immediate than it is right now. As we explore this biblical truth further in the coming chapters, may we gain a deeper longing for that glorious moment when our Savior splits the skies and calls us up to meet Him in the air.

Jesus told a parable in the gospel of Luke about servants who were waiting for their master to return from a wedding feast. These servants knew the master would be returning, but they didn't know exactly when. So Jesus said, "Stay dressed for action and keep your lamps burning, and be like men who are waiting for their master to come home from the wedding feast, so that they may open the door to him at once when he comes and knocks" (Luke 12:35–36).

In the same way, we should be like those watchful servants, always ready for our Master's return. We are to keep our lamps burning brightly through a life of prayer, obedience, and witness. We are to stay dressed for service, not entangled in the affairs of this world. We must live with a sense of expectancy, knowing that Jesus could come at any time.

Some Christians are so focused on their earthly lives and pursuits that they have lost sight of the Lord's imminent return. They are like the believers James addressed who were making business plans without any thought for the will of God. The apostle had to remind them,

> Come now, you who say, "Today or tomorrow we will go into such and such a town and spend a year there and trade and make a profit"—yet you do not know what tomorrow will bring. What is your life? For you are a mist that appears for a little time and then vanishes (James 4:13–14).

Since life is fleeting and Jesus can return at any time, James exhorted his readers:

> Instead you ought to say, "If the Lord wills, we will live and do this or that" (James 4:15).

We too must hold our earthly plans with a loose grip, submitting them to the Lordship of Jesus Christ, because He could return at any moment and interrupt our agenda with His Glorious Appearing. Like the believers in Thessalonica, we should be known as those who have turned from the empty pursuits of this world "to serve the living and true God and to wait for his Son from heaven" (1 Thessalonians 1:9–10).

Does that mean we should just sit around gazing at the sky? Not at all. The knowledge of Christ's imminent return should spur us to action, not idleness. Remember what Jesus told His disciples in the parable of the talents. The master entrusted his servants with various resources to invest for his benefit while he was gone. The wise servants put their talents to work and earned a profit for their master. The foolish servant buried his talent in the ground and earned nothing.

When the master returned, he commended the faithful servants:

> "'Well done, good and faithful servant. You have been faithful over a little; I will set you over much. Enter into the joy of your master'" (Matthew 25:21, 23).

But he rebuked the wicked and lazy servant and cast him into outer darkness (v. 30). The point is clear: the Lord has entrusted each of us with time, talents, and treasure to invest for His glory until He returns. One day, we will stand before Him to give an account of how we used what He gave us.

So the Rapture is not an excuse for passivity but a motivation for diligent service. Like the faithful servants, we should be busy about our Master's business, seeking to multiply our talents for His maximum glory. We shouldn't be like the scoffers who say, "Where is the promise of his coming?" and use the delay as a license to indulge our flesh (2 Peter 3:3–4). Instead, we should live in holiness and godliness.

> Since all these things are thus to be dissolved, what sort of people ought you to be in lives of holiness and godliness, waiting for and hastening the coming of the day of God, because of which the heavens will be set on fire and dissolved, and the heavenly bodies will melt as they burn! But according to his promise we are waiting for new heavens and a new earth in which righteousness dwells (2 Peter 3:11–13).

As this wicked world grows darker and the birth pains increase in both frequency and intensity, we can take heart that our redemption is drawing near. The Rapture is on the horizon. Jesus is coming soon. The night is far spent. The Day is at hand. So let us cast off the works of darkness and put on the armor of light. Let us walk properly, as in the day, eagerly waiting for our Blessed Hope, the Glorious Appearing of our great God and Savior Jesus Christ (Romans 13:11–14; Titus 2:13).

Even with the clear biblical evidence for the Rapture, some people still raise objections and questions. They may argue that the word "rapture" isn't found in the Bible or claim that it promotes escapism. In the next chapter, we will address these common critiques and demonstrate from Scripture why the Rapture is a vital doctrine for every believer. In the next chapter, we'll see that far from being an invention of modern prophecy teachers, the truth of the Rapture has been cherished by Christians throughout Church history. So if you have doubts or concerns about this teaching, keep reading as we respond to the major challenges to the Rapture.

2

Answering Rapture Objections

In the previous chapter, we defined the Rapture and distinguished it from the Second Coming of Christ. We saw that the Rapture is the next great event on God's prophetic calendar—an imminent event that requires no new signs. Jesus will descend from Heaven, resurrect deceased Church-Age believers, and catch up living believers to meet Him in the air and take them to the Father's House. The Rapture is the Blessed Hope that we as Christians should be eagerly anticipating.

Five Common Objections

However, despite the clear biblical evidence for the Rapture, many people raise objections and questions about this doctrine. Some claim the Rapture is not taught in the Bible at all. Others argue it is a recent invention. And some say it promotes an escapist mentality among believers. As teachers of God's Word, we want to directly address these objections so you can have full confidence in the truth of the Rapture. Let's examine five the most common criticisms and provide solid biblical responses.

1. The word "Rapture" is not in the Bible.

One of the first objections often raised is that the word "rapture" does not appear anywhere in the Bible. Critics argue that since this specific term is not found in Scripture, the doctrine must be non-biblical. However, this argument is flawed. Just because an exact word is not used does not mean the concept is not present.

Consider other terms not in the Bible, such as the word "trinity." The doctrine of the Father, Son, and Holy Spirit as three Persons yet One God is clearly taught. The word "millennium" doesn't appear either, but the concept of Christ's 1,000-year reign is unmistakably described in Revelation 20:1–7. Likewise, while the English word "rapture" may not be in most translations, the Greek word *harpazō* (which means 'to seize,' 'carry off by force,' or 'to snatch away') is used in key Rapture passages like 1 Thessalonians 4:17.

This word is also used to describe Philip being "caught away" by the Spirit after baptizing the Ethiopian eunuch (Acts 8:39). Later in 2 Corinthians 12:2–4, Paul says he was "caught up to the third heaven," using the same term *harpazō*. We find it again in Revelation 12:5 depicting the male child (Jesus) being "caught up" to God's Throne. So while the exact word "rapture" is not used, the idea is clearly conveyed by the Greek verb *harpazō* in these passages about the catching away of the Church.

Additionally, the earliest Latin translation of the Bible (the Latin Vulgate from around AD 400) used a form of the word *rapio* or *rapturo (rapiemur)* to translate *harpazō* in 1 Thessalonians 4:17. *Rapio* is the root of the English word "rapture" and conveys the same sudden, abrupt snatching or catching away seen in the Greek. So the biblical concept of the Rapture has been there from the beginning, even if the actual English word was not used until much later.

2. The Rapture is a recent invention.

As pastors and teachers of Bible prophecy, we've often encountered the claim that the Rapture is a recent invention, supposedly dreamed up by John Nelson Darby in the 1830s and not taught in the early Church or by the apostles. This accusation is frequently used to discredit the doctrine of the pre-Tribulation Rapture. One website critical of the Rapture states: "Rapture doctrine did not exist before John Darby invented it in 1830 AD. Before it 'popped into John Darby's head' no one had ever heard of a secret rapture."[1] This claim, while frequently repeated by Rapture critics, is demonstrably false. The Rapture, far from being a modern invention, has roots that stretch back to the early days of Christianity.[2]

The Early Church and the Rapture

When we look at the writings of the early church fathers, we find clear evidence that they understood and taught the core aspects of the Rapture. These early Christian leaders spoke about the removal of the Church before a coming time of tribulation. For instance, Irenaeus, who lived AD 130–202, wrote about believers being "caught up" to Heaven before the Tribulation:

> And therefore, when in the end the Church shall be suddenly caught up from this, it is said, *"There shall be tribulation such as has not been since the beginning, neither shall be."* Matthew 24:21 For this is the last contest of the righteous, in which, when they overcome they are crowned with incorruption.[3]

Irenaeus wasn't just any early Christian writer—he was a disciple of Polycarp, who in turn was a disciple of the apostle John himself. This connection brings us remarkably close to the apostolic age.

Eusebius of Caesarea was a Christian apologist who is also commonly known as the first significant church historian outside of the New Testament era. He lived from around AD 260 to May 30, 339. He used a pre-Tribulation image of a heavenly ark to illustrate the Rapture:

> Indeed, as all perished then except those gathered with Noah in the ark, so also at his coming, the ungodly in the season of apostasy ... shall perish.... At the time

of the deluge, it (judgment) did not come and destroy all the inhabitants of the earth before (until) Noah entered into the ark. Therefore, in the same way, at the consummation of the age, it (this pattern) says (demands) that the cataclysm of the destruction of the ungodly shall not happen before those men who are found of God at that time are gathered into the ark and saved according to the pattern of Noah ... all the righteous and godly are to be separated from the ungodly and gathered into the heavenly ark of God. For in this way [comes the time] when not even one righteous man will be found any more among mankind. And when all the ungodly have been made atheists by the antichrist, and the whole world is overcome by apostasy, the wrath of God shall come upon the ungodly.[4]

Another striking example comes from Ephraem the Syrian, a prominent teacher who lived from AD 306 to 373. In one of his essays, he wrote:

For all the saints and elect of God are gathered, prior to the Tribulation that is to come, and are taken to the Lord lest they see the confusion that is to overwhelm the world because of our sins.[5]

Notice the clear reference here to believers being gathered to the Lord before the coming Tribulation—a remarkably explicit description of the pre-Tribulation Rapture!

Ephraem wasn't alone in this belief. Other early church leaders like Hippolytus of Rome

(AD 170–236) and Cyprian of Carthage (AD 200–258) also wrote about believers being taken to Heaven before the time of Antichrist's appearance.

Similar references to the catching away of the saints before the Tribulation or the coming of Antichrist can be found in *The Shepherd of Hermas* (AD 140), as well as in the writings of Barnabas (AD 100), Tertullian (AD 200) and Lactantius (AD 310). There is simply no truth to the claim that no one believed in the Rapture before the 1800s. Belief in the catching up of the Church prior to the Tribulation has been around since the earliest days of Christianity.

The Middle Ages and Renaissance

As we move into the Middle Ages, we continue to find references to the Rapture. In the 14th century, a group known as the Apostolic Brethren in northern Italy believed they would be "transferred into paradise" and preserved from the Antichrist. Their leader, Brother Dolcino, used the Latin word *transferrentur* to describe this event—the same word medieval Christians used to describe Enoch's rapture or transference to Heaven.

The Protestant Reformation brought renewed interest in Bible prophecy. While the major reformers like John Calvin and Martin Luther were primarily focused on other doctrinal issues, Calvin did teach about the imminence of Christ's return. In his commentary on 1 Thessalonians, Calvin encouraged believers to be prepared for Christ's return at any moment.

The 17th and 18th Centuries: A Flowering of Rapture Doctrine

Contrary to what many believe, the 17th and 18th centuries saw a significant development in Rapture theology. Many prominent Christian leaders and scholars of this period wrote extensively about the Rapture, often in ways that closely resemble modern pre-Tribulation teachings.

Joseph Mede (1586–1638), a respected biblical scholar, wrote about Christ coming in the clouds to take up His saints, leaving the wicked behind on earth. Increase Mather (1639–1723), a prominent Puritan leader in colonial America, taught that Christ would come to rapture the saints before returning to earth for judgment.

Peter Jurieu, a French Huguenot pastor writing in 1687, described a Rapture where the saints will be carried up into the clouds to their Redeemer. John Gill, an influential Baptist theologian, wrote in 1748 about the Rapture being sudden, with saints caught up to meet the Lord in the air.

One of the clearest pre-Darby statements of a pre-Tribulation Rapture comes from Morgan Edwards (1722–1795), a Baptist minister who helped found Brown University. While still a student in the 1740s, Edwards wrote an essay proposing the Rapture of believers about three and a half years before the start of the Millennium:

> *The distance between the first and second resurrection will be somewhat more than a thousand years.*

I say, somewhat more, because the dead saints will be raised, and the living changed at Christ's "appearing in the air" (I Thes. iv, 17); and this will be about three years and a half before the millennium, as we shall see hereafter: but will he and they abide in the air all that time? No: they will ascend to paradise, or to some one of those many "mansions in the father's house of God" (John xiv: 2).[6]

The Concept of Dispensations

It's worth noting that the idea of dispensations—different periods in God's dealings with humanity—also has roots long before Darby. As early as 1647, Thomas Manton suggested four "dispensations" in God's plan.[7] William Sherwin, writing in 1675, elaborated on this concept, calling these periods "God's economy."[8] Even the Quaker William Penn wrote about various "dispensations of God" in history.[9]

The Rapture in America

The concept of the Rapture found fertile ground in America. Increase Mather, whom we mentioned earlier, published *The Blessed Hope, and the Glorious Appearing of the Great God Our Saviour, Jesus Christ* in 1701. In this work, he taught that Christ would first take believers to Heaven before returning with them to earth.

Even Jonathan Edwards, better known for his role in the Great Awakening and often associated with postmillennialism, believed in a Rapture before the

Final Judgment. His description of this event is both beautiful and sobering:

> Upon this, Christ and all his saints, and all the holy angels ministering to them, shall leave this lower world, and ascend towards the highest heavens.... He shall ascend with his elect church with him, glorified in body and soul.... The redeemed church shall all ascend with him in a most joyful and triumphant manner: and all their enemies and persecutors, who shall be left behind to be consumed.[10]

The Truth About Darby

So where does John Nelson Darby fit into all of this? It's true that Darby played a significant role in systematizing and popularizing pre-Tribulation Rapture doctrine in the 19th century. However, he absolutely did not invent it. What Darby did was take these long-existing ideas and organize them into a cohesive theological system that we now call dispensationalism.

Darby's work was influential, no doubt, but he was building on a foundation laid by centuries of Christian thinkers before him. The basic concepts he worked with had been circulating in England since the 16th century, and on the European continent for even longer.

Why This History Matters

You might be wondering why we are spending so much time on this history. Understanding the historical roots of the Rapture doctrine is crucial for several reasons:

1. It refutes the claim that the Rapture is a recent invention, giving the doctrine more credibility.

2. It shows that many godly men and women throughout church history have held to this belief.

3. It demonstrates that the idea of the Rapture emerges naturally from a careful study of Scripture, as evidenced by its recurring appearance throughout church history.

The Rapture Today

Today, the concept of the Rapture continues to be a source of hope and expectation for many believers. While there are different views on its timing (pre-Tribulation, mid-Tribulation, or post-Tribulation), the core idea of Christ returning for His Church remains a central part of Christian eschatology (teaching about the End Times).

As we look at the world around us, with its increasing turmoil and moral decay, the promise of the Rapture becomes ever more precious. The next time someone tells you that the Rapture is a recent invention, you can confidently explain that this simply isn't true. The Rapture, far from being a 19th-century innovation, has been a part of Christian teaching since the earliest days of the Church. From the Apostolic Fathers to the medieval mystics, from the Protestant reformers to the American Puritans, the hope of Christ's sudden return for His Church has inspired and encouraged believers for two thousand years.

3. The Rapture promotes escapism.

Perhaps the most common criticism of the Rapture doctrine is that it encourages an "escapist" mentality among Christians. Those who level this charge claim that belief in the Rapture makes believers apathetic and lazy, causing them to withdraw from society and neglect their responsibilities. "If we are just going to be taken to Heaven," they say, "then why bother getting involved in politics, culture, or meeting the needs of the world?"

At first glance, this argument may seem to have some merit. After all, if we believe Jesus could Rapture us at any moment, it might be tempting to just sit around and wait for His return instead of actively serving Him. However, this objection falls apart under closer biblical scrutiny. A belief in the Rapture, properly understood, does not produce laziness or apathy but rather the exact opposite. The New Testament repeatedly teaches that the promise of Christ's imminent return should spur us to greater holiness, diligence, and evangelistic urgency.

Consider what the apostle John wrote in 1 John 3:2–3, right after mentioning the appearing of Christ:

> Beloved, we are God's children now, and what we will be has not yet appeared; but we know that when he

> appears we shall be like him, because we shall see him
> as he is. And everyone who thus hopes in him purifies
> himself as he is pure.

Notice that John says the hope of Christ's appearing should motivate us to purity and Christlikeness. If we really believe Jesus could come back at any moment, it ought to make us want to be living in a way that pleases Him. We should be walking closely with the Lord, confessing sin, growing in godliness, and being conformed to the image of Christ. The doctrine of imminency promotes personal holiness.

Or think of what Jesus said when speaking of His return in Luke 19:13: "Engage in business until I come." Jesus expects His followers to stay busy serving Him and extending His Kingdom until He returns.

Jesus told a parable to illustrate this principle in Matthew 24:45–51. He spoke of two types of servants: one faithful and sensible, the other evil. The faithful servant kept doing his master's will during the master's absence. He continued feeding the other servants and fulfilling his duties. But the evil servant used the delay in the master's return as an excuse for sinful living and irresponsibility. When the master returned, the faithful servant was rewarded, and the evil servant was punished. The lesson is clear: the possibility of the master's soon return should motivate the servants to diligence and faithfulness, not laziness and sin.

So it is with the Rapture. Knowing that our Lord could appear at any moment to catch us up to Heaven is the greatest incentive for holy living and urgent ministry. Like the faithful servant, we should stay busy doing our Master's will until He comes. We must not use the delay in His coming as an excuse for ungodliness but as a mandate for obedience.

Paul presented the Rapture as a source of great comfort and encouragement to suffering believers. After describing the catching up of the saints in 1 Thessalonians 4, he concluded by saying, "Therefore encourage one another with these words" (v. 18).

In other translations Paul tells the believers to "comfort one another." How is the Rapture an encouragement and a comfort? It reminds us that our present sufferings and trials are not worthy to be compared to the glory that awaits us (Romans 8:18). It assures us that no matter what happens, we have a secure hope in Heaven. Jesus is coming to take us to be with Himself in the Father's house (John 14:1–3). Focusing on the Rapture helps us live with an eternal perspective.

Belief in the Rapture also promotes faithful evangelism and gospel preaching. If we really believe Christ could return at any moment, it should fuel our efforts to reach the lost before it is too late. We know that those left behind will enter the Tribulation period, the most terrible time in human history. Knowing what lies in store for unbelievers should create a sense of urgency to share the gospel with as many as possible before Jesus comes.

Think of Paul's heart for his fellow Jews who had rejected the gospel. He wrote,

> Brothers, my heart's desire and prayer to God for them is that they may be saved (Romans 10:1).

Paul was willing to give himself up to eternal damnation if it meant his fellow Jews could be saved (Romans 9:3). He viewed himself as under obligation to preach the gospel (Romans 1:14). The fact that sinners could be left behind at the Rapture to face the horrors of the Tribulation should motivate us to even greater efforts in pursuing the Great Commission before Jesus splits the skies.

So to summarize, the common objection that the Rapture promotes escapism and laziness simply does not match up with what the Bible actually teaches. Scripture repeatedly presents the Rapture as a motivation to godly living and diligent service:

- It purifies our lives as we prepare to meet Christ (1 John 3:2–3).

- It motivates us to engage in business until He comes (Luke 19:13).

- It comforts and encourages us and gives us an eternal perspective (1 Thessalonians 4:18).

- It produces an evangelistic urgency to reach the lost (Romans 10:1).

Rather than causing us to withdraw from the world, the Rapture should energize us to maximize our time and make the most of every opportunity to serve Christ. Properly understood, this doctrine inspires responsibility and readiness for Christ's return, not irresponsibility.

4. The Rapture divides the Second Coming into two phases.

Some believers who reject the Rapture argue that it wrongly divides the Second Coming of Christ into two events—the Rapture before the Tribulation and the Glorious Appearing after the Tribulation. They claim the Bible only speaks of one "second coming," so it is unbiblical to separate the catching up of the saints from Christ's return to earth after the Tribulation.

In response, we need to acknowledge that most Bible-believing Christians do see the Second Coming as a single event. It is true that Scripture does not explicitly state there will be stages or phases of the Second Coming: the Rapture followed by a "the Glorious Appearing." However, the details given in biblical prophecy make a two-phase Second Coming not only possible but necessary to harmonize all of the biblical data.

Consider that there are two different pictures painted of Christ's return in the Bible. The first picture is given by Jesus Himself in John 14:1–3. On the night before His crucifixion, He told His disciples that He was going to His Father's house to prepare a place for them. Then He said,

> "And if I go and prepare a place for you, I will come again and will take you to myself, that where I am you may be also" (v. 3).

Notice some key elements of Jesus' promise:

- Jesus is going to the Father's House (later revealed as the New Jerusalem).

- He is going there to prepare a place for believers.

- He will come again to receive His followers to Himself.

- He will take them to be where He is in the Father's House.

In John 14, we have a depiction of Christ coming for His saints (the Rapture) to take them to Heaven to be with Him. But in numerous other places, we see Christ coming with His saints to execute judgment on the ungodly and set up His earthly kingdom. For example:

> And you shall flee to the valley of my mountains, for the valley of the mountains shall reach to Azal. And you shall flee as you fled from the earthquake in the days of Uzziah king of Judah. Then the LORD my God will come, and all the holy ones with him (Zechariah 14:5).

And to grant relief to you who are afflicted as well as to us, when the Lord Jesus is revealed from heaven with his mighty angels in flaming fire, inflicting vengeance on those who do not know God and on those who do not obey the gospel of our Lord Jesus (2 Thessalonians 1:7–8).

It was also about these that Enoch, the seventh from Adam, prophesied, saying, "Behold, the Lord comes with ten thousands of his holy ones, to execute judgment on all and to convict all the ungodly of all their deeds of ungodliness that they have committed in such an ungodly way, and of all the harsh things that ungodly sinners have spoken against him" (Jude 14–15).

And the armies of heaven, arrayed in fine linen, white and pure, were following him on white horses. From his mouth comes a sharp sword with which to strike down the nations, and he will rule them with a rod of iron. He will tread the winepress of the fury of the wrath of God the Almighty (Revelation 19:14–15).

In these passages, Christ is not coming alone for His saints as He is in John 14, but rather He is coming from Heaven to earth with His saints to pour out judgment on the wicked. It is difficult to see how these two very different depictions of Christ's coming could be reconciled as describing the same singular event. They must be speaking of two different phases of His return, even if not explicitly called such.

A careful analysis of Christ's Second Coming prophecies reveals numerous differences in the biblical details:

Rapture

- Christ comes for His saints (John 14:3; 1 Thessalonians 4:16–17).

- Believers meet Christ in the air (1 Thessalonians 4:17).

- Christ takes believers to Heaven (John 14:3).

- The world is not judged but enters the Tribulation.

- It occurs before the Day of Wrath (1 Thessalonians 5:9; Revelation 3:10).

- It is a message of hope and comfort (1 Thessalonians 4:18; Titus 2:13).

- It can happen at any moment (1 Thessalonians 5:2; Revelation 3:3).

- Only believers will see Jesus (1 Corinthians 15:52; 1 Thessalonians 4:17).

Second Coming (Glorious Appearing)

- Christ comes with His saints (Zechariah 14:5; Revelation 19:14).

- Christ's feet touch the earth (Zechariah 14:4; Revelation 19:11–12).

- Christ establishes His Kingdom on earth (Matthew 25:31–32).

- The world is judged and righteousness established (Revelation 19:15).

- It occurs after the Tribulation at the end of the Day of the Lord.

- It is a message of judgment and wrath (Jude 14–15; 2 Thessalonians 1:7–10).

- It follows many events/signs that must happen first (Matthew 24:29–30).

- Every eye will see Jesus (Matthew 24:30; Revelation 1:7).

When we carefully compare the details between these two phases of Christ's return, it becomes clear that they must be describing distinct events, even if not specifically called a "two-stage coming." Just as Christ came the first time in two phases—first at His incarnation (birth) and later at His triumphal entry—so He will come again in two phases: first for His saints at the Rapture and later with His saints at the Glorious Appearing. Seeing Christ's return as consisting of these two aspects brings the greatest harmony to the prophetic Scriptures.

5. There is no mention of the Resurrection or Rapture in Revelation chapters 4–22.

One final objection to the pre-Tribulation Rapture has to do with the book of Revelation. Some argue that if the Rapture will happen before the Tribulation period, which is described in Revelation chapters 6–19, then we would expect to see clear mention of the Resurrection and Rapture in Revelation chapters 4–5, which describe the heavenly scene just prior to the Tribulation. Since no explicit reference to the Rapture is found in those chapters, then the Rapture must not occur before the Tribulation.

In response to this objection, it's important to remember that the book of Revelation is not written in a strict chronological sequence, although there is a general chronological outline. After the Letters to the Seven Churches in chapters 2–3, John is caught up to the throne room of Heaven in chapter 4. From that point on, the Revelation alternates between events happening in Heaven and events happening on the earth, often covering the same ground from different perspectives.

Furthermore, while no explicit mention of the Resurrection or Rapture appears in Revelation chapters 4–5, there are clues that the Raptured Church is in view. In Revelation 4:1, John hears a trumpet-like voice saying, "Come up here," and he is instantly translated from earth to Heaven. Many see this as a picture of the Rapture of the Church occurring before the Tribulation begins. The fact that the 24 elders, who may represent the Raptured Church, are already in Heaven before the Tribulation supports this conclusion.

Additionally, Revelation chapters 4–5 describe a heavenly scene of universal worship and praise around the Throne of God. The focus is on the Lamb who was slain purchasing people from every tribe, tongue, and nation to be a kingdom and priests to God (Revelation 5:8–10). This is likely a reference to the Church, the bride of Christ, which sings a new song of praise to the Lamb for His redemptive work. The Church is pictured in Heaven before the seals are opened in chapter 6, which launches the beginning of the Tribulation period.

So while Revelation chapters 4–5 may not have explicit statements about the Resurrection or Rapture, the clues are there that the Church is already in Heaven before God's wrath is poured out on the earth. The absence of the Church from the events on earth described in Revelation chapters 6–19 also implies that the Church is not present during the Tribulation but rather has been raptured to Heaven beforehand.

Putting It All Together

In this chapter, we have sought to address some of the most common objections and questions about the Rapture. We have shown that:

- The concept of the Rapture is clearly taught in Scripture using words like "caught up" and "snatched away," even if the English word "rapture" does not appear.

- The Rapture is not a recent invention of John Nelson Darby in the 1800s but has been taught in various forms by Church leaders since the early centuries of Christianity.

- The Rapture does not promote escapism or spiritual laziness but is actually one of the greatest motivations for holy living, evangelism, and ministry.

- The biblical details demand that the Second Coming of Christ be viewed in two stages: the Rapture before the Tribulation and the Return (Glorious Appearing) after the Tribulation.

- While not mentioned explicitly, the clues are present in Revelation chapters 4–5 that the Church has already been caught up to Heaven to be with Christ before the Tribulation begins.

Of course, there are many other objections and questions that could be raised about the Rapture. But hopefully this treatment of five of the most common criticisms has helped strengthen your understanding of and confidence in this supernatural event. As we'll see in the next chapter, the timing of the Rapture in relation to the Tribulation and Millennium is a key issue that must be carefully addressed. May we be like the Bereans who searched the Scriptures daily to see if these things are true (Acts 17:11).

3

The Timing of the Rapture

So far, we have laid the groundwork by defining the Rapture and distinguishing it from the Second Coming. We saw that the Rapture is the next great event on God's prophetic calendar, where Jesus will descend from Heaven, resurrect Church-Age believers who have died and catch up living believers to meet Him in the air. Then, in Chapter 2, we addressed common objections to the Rapture, demonstrating that the concept is clearly taught in Scripture, has been believed throughout Church history, and is meant to motivate us to holy living and urgent ministry, not spiritual laziness or escapism.

Now, as we build on that foundation, we come to one of the most debated aspects of the Rapture doctrine: the specific timing or chronology in relation to the seven-year Tribulation period. When will this momentous event occur? Will the Church be raptured before the Tribulation, in the middle of it, or at the end when Jesus returns? These are important questions that significantly impact how we view the End Times and live our lives in light of Christ's coming.

When Will the Rapture Happen?—Four Views

When it comes to the timing of the Rapture, there are four main views held by Bible-believing Christians today:

1. **Pre-Tribulation Rapture:** The Rapture will occur before the seven-year Tribulation begins.

2. **Mid-Tribulation Rapture:** The Rapture will occur at the midpoint of the seven-year Tribulation.

3. **Pre-Wrath Rapture:** The Rapture will occur sometime after the midpoint of the Tribulation but before the Bowl Judgments (the wrath of God) are poured out on the earth.

4. **Post-Tribulation Rapture:** The Rapture will occur at the end of the seven-year Tribulation, in conjunction with the Second Coming of Christ.

Each of these views has arguments to support its position. As we navigate these perspectives, it is crucial to maintain a firm commitment to the authority of God's Word and to allow Scripture to interpret Scripture. While we may hold differing views on the chronology of the Rapture, we must never compromise the fundamental truths of the Rapture and Christ's promised return. That said, we believe that when you examine the Scriptures closely and consistently, the pre-Tribulation Rapture position is the most biblically supported view. Let's look at each of the other positions before presenting the case for the pre-Tribulation view.

Mid-Tribulation Rapture View

The mid-Tribulation view sees the Rapture occurring at the midpoint of the seven-year period. Mid-Tribulation proponents often identify the last trumpet of 1 Corinthians 15:52 with the seventh Trumpet Judgment of Revelation 11. They believe the Church will go through the first 3.5 years of the Tribulation but be spared the more severe judgments of the second half (the Great Tribulation).

However, we believe the pre-Tribulation view better explains the differences between the trumpet of 1 Corinthians 15 and the Trumpet Judgments in Revelation. The last trumpet in 1 Corinthians 15 is called "the trumpet of God" (1 Thessalonians 4:16). It signals the close of the Church Age and gathers believers to the Lord. But the Trumpet Judgments in Revelation are sounded by angels and unleash divine wrath on the unbelieving world. They are different events for different purposes.

Pre-Wrath Rapture View

The pre-wrath view has gained some popularity recently. It agrees with the pre-Tribulation view that the Church is exempt from divine wrath but sees the wrath as beginning sometime after the midpoint of the Tribulation. Pre-wrath advocates distinguish between the persecution of the Antichrist in the first half and the wrath of God in the second half. They usually place the Rapture around the sixth Seal Judgment of Revelation 6.

But we find several problems with the pre-wrath position. It fails to see that the entire seven-year period is the "Seventieth week of Daniel," a time when God's wrath is being poured out on a Christ-rejecting world. While the judgments escalate in severity through the Tribulation, they all proceed from the Throne of God as the Lamb opens the seals (Revelation chapters 5–6). The pre-wrath view also struggles to reconcile the New Testament teaching of imminency with the definite signs and events required to precede the Rapture in their scheme.

Post-Tribulation Rapture View

The post-Tribulation view holds that the Rapture and Second Coming are facets of a single event at the end of the Tribulation. Jesus will return at the conclusion of Daniel's Seventieth Week to resurrect believers who have died, rapture the living ones, and immediately descend to earth to establish His Millennial Kingdom. Proponents of a post-Tribulation Rapture draw a strong distinction between Satan's wrath, which the Church may suffer, and God's wrath, from which we are promised deliverance. They argue passages about Christ's coming don't necessitate a pre-Tribulation Rapture.

One of the main arguments for this view is that the Church needs to be raptured at the end so we can immediately return with Christ to earth. But this fails to account for the biblical events that occur between the Rapture and Second Coming: the Judgment Seat of Christ and the Marriage Supper of the Lamb. It also does not address why the Church is never mentioned on earth in Revelation chapters 6–18 or why the Second Coming is preceded by specific signs while the Rapture is sign-less (without warning) and imminent.

The Case for the pre-Tribulation Rapture

While we respect our brothers and sisters who hold these other views, we believe the cumulative biblical case points most convincingly to the pre-Tribulation view. This position that the Rapture will occur before the Tribulation period begins, removing the Church prior to this time of unprecedented judgment, has been the dominant view among many scholars, churches, and Christians, especially in the last two centuries. Here are nine key biblical arguments for the pre-Tribulation position:

1. The Church is promised exemption from divine wrath.

One of the clearest biblical reasons for the pre-Tribulation Rapture is the promise that believers will not face the wrath of God. Paul assures us in 1 Thessalonians 1:10 that we are waiting for God's Son from Heaven: "Jesus who delivers us from the wrath to come." The apostle reiterates truth in 1 Thessalonians 5:9: "For God has not destined us for wrath, but to obtain salvation through our Lord Jesus Christ." In Romans 5:9, he also states, "Since, therefore, we have now been justified by his blood, much more shall we be saved by him from the wrath of God." The book of Revelation clearly portrays the Tribulation as a time of God's wrath being poured out on the world (Revelation 6:16–17; 11:18; 14:10, 19; 15:1, 7; 16:1, 19). If the Church goes through the Tribulation, then these promises of deliverance from wrath seem meaningless.

2. The Rapture is presented as imminent.

Throughout the New Testament, the Rapture is consistently presented as an imminent event that could happen at any moment. Believers are exhorted to watch and be ready for the Lord's coming (Matthew 24:42, 44; 25:13; 1 Thessalonians 5:6). The early church lived with a constant expectation of Christ's return (1 Thessalonians 1:9–10; 1 Corinthians 1:7; Philippians 3:20; Titus 2:13; James 5:7–9; 1 Peter 4:7; Jude 21; Revelation 22:20).

Only the pre-Tribulation position allows for the Rapture to be truly imminent. If the Rapture is mid-Tribulation, pre-wrath, or Post-Tribulation, then certain prophesied events must happen before it occurs, making it impossible for Christ to return at any moment. With a pre-Tribulation Rapture, no prophecies remain to be fulfilled before Christ can come. He could return today, tomorrow, or anytime—just as the Scripture indicates.

3. The Church is missing on earth during the Tribulation.

One of the most striking pieces of evidence for a pre-Tribulation Rapture is the absence of the Church in Revelation chapters 6–18, the chapters that detail the Tribulation period. The Church is repeatedly mentioned in Revelation chapters 1–3, but then it disappears until the end of the book. In total, the Church is referred 19 times in the first three chapters, but then it is not mentioned even once by name in chapters 6–18. The Church reappears at the end of Revelation 19, as the bride of Christ returns with Him to earth. The implication seems obvious: the Church is in Heaven during the Tribulation events of Revelation chapters 6–18.

Furthermore, the outline of Revelation supports a pre-Tribulation Rapture. In Revelation 1:19, John is told to write what he has seen, what currently is (the Church Age), and what will happen after these things (the events of Revelation chapters 4–22). The Greek phrase *meta tauta*, meaning 'after these things,' is used in Revelation 4:1 where John (a picture of the Church) is called to Heaven ("Come up here") to see the future events. This "catch up" call in Revelation 4:1 is parallel to Paul's "caught up" language for the Rapture in 1 Thessalonians 4:17. After Revelation 4:1, the Church is not seen on earth again until the end of the Tribulation, implying the Church has already been raptured to Heaven.

4. The 24 Elders represent the Raptured Church.

Revelation chapters 4–5 picture a heavenly throne room with 24 elders sitting on thrones around God's Throne. Most likely, these elders represent the Raptured Church. They are wearing the white robes and victor's crowns (Greek: *stephanos*) promised to the overcoming Church in Revelation 2:10 and 3:4–5. The fact that they are seen in Heaven before the Tribulation begins in Revelation chapter 6 indicates that the Rapture and the Bema Judgment of believers has already happened.

Who are these elders? They can't be angels because angels are never numbered or crowned. If they are humans, then they must be glorified saints in resurrected bodies. But no one was resurrected or glorified before Christ, and no other resurrections are mentioned as occurring before this time. The most logical conclusion is that the 24 elders represent the Church that has been caught up to Heaven and rewarded prior to the Tribulation.

5. The Restrainer must be removed before the Antichrist is revealed.

In 2 Thessalonians chapter 2, Paul says a certain "restrainer" is holding back the revelation of the Antichrist. Only when this restraining force is removed can the "lawless one" be revealed. Most pre-Millennial scholars identify this "restrainer" as the Holy Spirit working through the Church to restrain evil. For the Antichrist to be revealed, then, the Church must first be removed via the Rapture. No other view can adequately explain the identity and removal of this Restrainer before the Antichrist's unveiling.

6. There is a biblical pattern of God delivering His people from wrath.

Throughout the Bible, God consistently delivers the righteous before pouring out judgment on the ungodly. He rescued Noah before the Flood, Lot before Sodom and Gomorrah's destruction, and Rahab before Jericho fell. These well-known examples create a precedent that God will continue with the Church. The fact that the Church is promised deliverance from the "hour of trial" in Revelation 3:10 fits this pattern. We believe the Church will be removed before the seven-year Tribulation, which is the "time of Jacob's trouble" focused on Israel (Jeremiah 30:7; Daniel 9:24).

7. The Jewish marriage analogy supports a pre-Tribulation Rapture.

The relationship between Christ and the Church is depicted in Scripture as a bride and groom (2 Corinthians 11:2; Ephesians 5:25–27; Revelation 19:7–9). In the Jewish wedding tradition, the groom would go to prepare a place for his bride, paralleling Christ's promise in John 14:2–3. Then, at an unexpected time, the groom would come for his bride and take her to his father's house for the wedding and wedding feast. This "snatching away" of the bride parallels the Rapture of the Church before the Wedding Feast in Heaven (the Judgment Seat of Christ and Marriage Supper of the Lamb). After the wedding feast, the bride would return with the groom to reign as king and queen of their home. This parallels the Church returning with Christ at the Second Coming.

If the Rapture doesn't happen until the end of the seven years, then either the wedding festivities must be very brief, or the Church's Marriage and Wedding Feast get mixed into the Millennium. A post-Tribulation Rapture doesn't fit the precision of the wedding analogy, which implies an interval of time between the groom receiving his bride and the couple returning in triumphant procession.

8. The Pre-Tribulation view allows for distinctions between Israel and the Church.

The book of Daniel predicts a seven-year period—the seventieth week of Daniel—in which God will complete His plan for Israel and the nations (Daniel 9:24–27). This time period is distinct from the Church Age, as evidenced by the fact that the Church was not involved in the first sixty-nine weeks. If the Church is on earth during the seventieth week, then God is dealing with Israel and the Church simultaneously, blurring the lines between the two. However, the pre-Tribulation view allows for a clear distinction between the Church Age and the "time of Jacob's trouble" focused on Israel's salvation and the judgment of unbelieving Gentile nations.

9. The Church isn't mentioned in passages about the Second Coming.

When Jesus and Paul give Tribulation signs and woes in the Olivet Discourse (Matthew chapters 24–25 and 2 Thessalonians chapter 2), they never mention the Rapture or the Church as involved in those end-times events. Instead, the context is exclusively Israel. If the Rapture doesn't occur until the end of the Tribulation, then why does Jesus never address the Church in His lengthy message about end-times signs? The most logical answer is that the Rapture has already happened before the seven-year period begins and the signs occur.

Similarly, in Revelation chapter 19, when Jesus returns from Heaven to earth, the Church returns with Him already dressed in fine linen and riding on white horses. But no mention is made of the Resurrection or Rapture of living believers at this time.

Why? Because the Church was already raptured and rewarded before the Tribulation started.

Some Final Clarifications

While we believe the evidence for a pre-Tribulation Rapture is strong and consistent, we recognize that good, Bible-believing Christians hold other views. It's important to emphasize that the Rapture is not meant to be a point of division or arrogance. As we contend for this doctrine, several clarifications are in order.

First, belief in a pre-Tribulation Rapture is not based on a desire to escape suffering. Christians throughout history have suffered and been persecuted for their faith. Jesus promised that in this world we will have trouble (John 16:33). The Church won't be removed to avoid normal hardship but to be delivered from the unprecedented outpouring of God's eschatological wrath (1 Thessalonians 1:10, 5:9; Revelation 3:10).

Second, the pre-Tribulation view is not a recent invention of John Nelson Darby. While Darby did systematize and popularize this view, the concept of the Church being raptured before the Tribulation can be found in the early church fathers, medieval theologians, and the writings of those in the 1600s and 1700s.

What matters most is not when a doctrine was developed in Church history but whether that doctrine is taught in Scripture. We believe a face-value reading of biblical prophecy is most consistent with the pre-Tribulation position.

Finally, while we may not know the exact timing of the Rapture, we can know its nearness. The signs that Christ's return is approaching are evident and increasing. Whether He comes for us before, in the middle, or after the Tribulation, the crucial thing is to be ready. As we await our Blessed Hope, may we be diligent to live holy and godly lives, share the gospel urgently, and encourage one another with the promise of His appearing (Titus 2:11–14).

With the timing of the Rapture now clearly established as occurring before the seven-year Tribulation, we can turn our attention to the biblical foundation for this doctrine. In the next chapter, we'll dive deep into the passages that reveal the Rapture in both the Old and New Testaments. From types and shadows in the Old Testament to Jesus' own words and the apostles' teachings, we'll see how the Rapture is a consistent theme woven throughout the pages of Scripture. As we marvel at the unity and precision of God's prophetic plan, may our hearts overflow with excitement and anticipation for the day we see our Savior face-to-face!

4

The Bible and the Rapture

In the previous chapters, we have laid a solid foundation for understanding the Rapture. We began by defining this momentous event and distinguishing it from the Second Coming. We then addressed common objections to the Rapture, demonstrating that it is a biblical doctrine firmly rooted in Scripture. Finally, we examined the various views on the timing of the Rapture in relation to the Tribulation period, concluding that the pre-Tribulation position is most consistent with a face-value reading of the prophetic passages. With this groundwork in place, we now want to take a closer look at what the Bible itself teaches about the Rapture.

The doctrine of the Rapture is not based on just a few isolated proof texts but is progressively revealed throughout the pages of Scripture. From the Old Testament types and shadows to the teachings of Jesus and the apostles in the New Testament, the Bible paints a consistent and compelling picture of God's plan to deliver His people before the outpouring of His wrath on a Christ-rejecting world.

Old Testament Foreshadowings

While the word "rapture" is not found in the Old Testament or elsewhere in the Bible, the concept is foreshadowed through several key events that showcase God's pattern of delivering the righteous before pouring out judgment on the wicked.

Enoch's Translation (Genesis 5:21–24)

Enoch, the seventh generation from Adam, stands out as an extraordinary figure who walked with God and was suddenly taken to Heaven without experiencing death. Genesis 5:24 states, "Enoch walked with God, and he was not, for God took him."

The New Testament sheds more light on this event:

> By faith Enoch was taken up so that he should not see death, and he was not found, because God had taken him. Now before he was taken he was commended as having pleased God (Hebrews 11:5).

Many Bible scholars see Enoch's unique translation to Heaven as a foreshadowing of the Rapture, where believers will be instantly caught up to be with the Lord without tasting death.

Noah and the Flood (Genesis Chapters 6–8)

God graciously removed Noah and his family before the floodwaters of judgment came upon the earth. They were sealed inside the ark of safety while the unbelieving world perished. This is a vivid picture of how the Church will be kept from the coming "hour of trial" (Revelation 3:10) that will come upon the whole world during the Tribulation period.

Lot's Deliverance from Sodom (Genesis Chapter 19)

God supernaturally rescued Lot and his daughters from the imminent destruction of Sodom and Gomorrah. The angels urged them to escape for their lives and not look back, because judgment was about to rain down on the cities of the plain. Lot's removal from Sodom prior to its devastation by fire and brimstone is a clear type of the Church being snatched away from this world before the Tribulation begins.

Elijah's Translation (2 Kings 2:11–12)

The prophet Elijah was miraculously caught up to Heaven in a whirlwind accompanied by a chariot and horses of fire. His dramatic rapture bypassed death and foreshadows the future translation of living believers at the Rapture (1 Corinthians 15:51–52). It's interesting to note that Jewish tradition holds Elijah will return as a precursor to the Messiah, and some believe he may be one of the Two Witnesses mentioned in Revelation 11.

———

While not specifically describing the Rapture, these Old Testament examples reveal a consistent pattern in God's dealings: He delivers the righteous before executing judgment on the unbelieving world. This principle is carried into the New Testament with the promise that the Church will be kept from the coming wrath (1 Thessalonians 1:10; 5:9; Revelation 3:10).

Jesus' Teachings on His Return

When we come to the Gospels, we find the Lord Jesus Himself alluding to the Rapture. While He did not use the term "rapture," He spoke of a sudden, selective removal of people from the earth prior to a time of unprecedented judgment.

The Olivet Discourse
(Matthew Chapters 24–25)

Jesus' most extensive teaching on the End Times is known as the Olivet Discourse. He delivered this sermon on the Mount of Olives during the final week before His crucifixion. In it Jesus outlines the signs and events leading up to His return. In Matthew 24:36–44, Jesus compares His coming to the days of Noah and Lot, emphasizing the suddenness and unexpectedness of the event. He states that people will be going about business as usual when judgment comes:

> "For as in those days before the flood they were eating and drinking, marrying and giving in marriage,

until the day when Noah entered the ark, and they were unaware until the flood came and swept them all away, so will be the coming of the Son of Man" (Matthew 24:38–39).

But then, in the twinkling of an eye, "one will be taken and one left" (v. 40–41).

What does Jesus mean by "taken" and "left"? The Greek word *paralambano*, translated "taken," means to "receive or take to oneself." It's the same word used for the angels taking Lot out of Sodom:

> "Likewise, just as it was in the days of Lot—they were eating and drinking, buying and selling, planting and building, but on the day when Lot went out from Sodom, fire and sulfur rained from heaven and destroyed them all—so will it be on the day when the Son of Man is revealed" (Luke 17:28–29).

In contrast, the word for "left," *aphiemi,* often means to "abandon or forsake." So the picture is of Christ coming to take His own unto Himself, while the unbelieving world is left behind to face judgment—a perfect description of the Rapture!

The Upper Room Discourse (John 14:1–4)
On the night before His crucifixion, Jesus comforted His disciples with the promise of His return. He said,

> "Let not your hearts be troubled. Believe in God; believe also in me. In my Father's house are many

rooms. If it were not so, would I have told you that I go to prepare a place for you? And if I go and prepare a place for you, I will come again and will take you to myself, that where I am you may be also. And you know the way to where I am going" (John 14:1–4).

This is one of the clearest Rapture passages in the Gospels. Notice that Jesus says He will come again to "receive" believers to Himself, that we may be with Him where He is. His return here is not to reign on the earth (as it will be at the Second Coming) but to take His Church to the Father's House in Heaven. This "coming again" to gather believers unto Himself is distinct from His return at the end of the Tribulation. It's the Rapture of the Church!

Other Statements from Jesus

Jesus made several other intriguing statements that hint at the Rapture. In Luke, after describing the terrible events of the Tribulation, He said,

> "But stay awake at all times, praying that you may have strength to escape all these things that are going to take place, and to stand before the Son of Man" (Luke 21:36).

The word translated "escape" here means to "flee out of, seek safety in flight, or vanish"—a fitting description of the Rapture.

Similarly, in Revelation, the risen Christ makes this promise to the faithful church of Philadelphia:

"Because you have kept my word about patient endurance, I will keep you from the hour of trial that is coming on the whole world, to try those who dwell on the earth" (Revelation 3:10).

True believers will be kept out of the coming worldwide Tribulation period by being raptured to Heaven.

Paul's Revelation of the Rapture

Undoubtedly, the apostle Paul gives the most detailed and definitive information about the Rapture in the New Testament. Paul's revelation goes beyond anything previously written to describe the participants, the resurrection of the dead in Christ, the translation of the living, the reunion in the air, and the ultimate destination of the raptured saints.

An Explicit Description
(1 Thessalonians 4:13–18)
The first explicit mention of the Rapture in Scripture is found in a well-known passage from Paul's first letter to the Thessalonians, where Paul explains the fate of those believers who have died before Christ's return. He begins by stating that he does not want the Thessalonian believers to be ignorant about those who have "fallen asleep" (a euphemism for believers who have died). He assures them that the dead in Christ will not miss out on the Rapture but will actually precede the living:

But we do not want you to be uninformed, brothers, about those who are asleep, that you may not grieve as others do who have no hope. For since we believe that Jesus died and rose again, even so, through Jesus, God will bring with him those who have fallen asleep. For this we declare to you by a word from the Lord, that we who are alive, who are left until the coming of the Lord, will not precede those who have fallen asleep. For the Lord himself will descend from heaven with a cry of command, with the voice of an archangel, and with the sound of the trumpet of God. And the dead in Christ will rise first. Then we who are alive, who are left, will be caught up together with them in the clouds to meet the Lord in the air, and so we will always be with the Lord. Therefore encourage one another with these words (1 Thessalonians 4:13–18).

This passage provides a wealth of details about the Rapture that are found nowhere else in Scripture:

1. The Lord's Return
The Rapture will be initiated by Jesus Christ Himself. It's not the work of angels or impersonal forces but Christ personally coming for His bride, the Church.

2. The Accompanying Sounds
The Rapture will be a noisy, attention-grabbing event, at least for believers in Christ. It will be accompanied by a shout (likely the voice of Christ), the voice of the archangel (probably Michael), and the trumpet of God (not to be confused with the Trumpet Judgments in Revelation). These dramatic

sounds will signal the moment of the Rapture. The biblical text is not definitive that these sounds will be heard or understood by unbelievers, but believers will hear them just before meeting the Lord in the air.

3. The Resurrection of the Dead in Christ
Deceased believers will be resurrected first. They will not miss out on the Rapture but will in fact be given priority over those still living. This resurrection will reunite their glorified bodies with their spirits that have been in the presence of the Lord (2 Corinthians 5:8).

4. The Translation of the Living
Immediately following the resurrection of the dead, those believers who are alive at the Rapture will be "caught up" to meet the Lord in the air. As we noted earlier, the Greek word *harpazō*, translated "caught up," means to 'seize, carry off, snatch up.' It refers to a sudden, irresistible act of catching away.

5. The Reunion in the Air
All believers in Christ, both resurrected and translated, will be united with Christ in the air above the earth. The dead in Christ will have already received their resurrection bodies, while the living will experience an instantaneous change "in the twinkling of an eye" (1 Corinthians 15:51–52).

6.The Final Destination

From the moment of the Rapture, believers in Christ will "always be with the Lord." This speaks of the eternal state, where believers will forever be in the presence of Christ, first in Heaven and then in the New Jerusalem (Revelation chapters 21–22). What a glorious future awaits us!

One particularly interesting note: Paul says this revelation came as a direct "word from the Lord" (I Thessalonians 4:15). This means Paul received these truths about the Rapture from Jesus Himself, likely during his three-year stay in Arabia (Galatians 1:11–12, 15–18) or through some other divine revelation during Paul's ministry.

A Parallel Passage (1 Corinthians 15:51–57)

In this parallel passage to 1 Thessalonians 4, Paul discusses the Rapture in 1 Corinthians in relation to the resurrection and the believer's glorified body. He begins by stating, "Behold, I tell you a mystery" (1 Corinthians 15:51). In the Bible, a "mystery" refers to truth previously hidden but now revealed. The complete picture of the Rapture was a "secret" God revealed to Paul that had not been fully known before.

Paul then describes what will take place at the Rapture:

> We shall not all sleep, but we shall all be changed, in a moment, in the twinkling of an eye, at the last trumpet. For the trumpet will sound, and the dead

will be raised imperishable, and we shall be changed (1 Corinthians 15:51–52).

The key word here is "changed." At the Rapture, living believers will be transformed instantly from their mortal, corruptible bodies to immortal, incorruptible bodies. Paul explains that "flesh and blood cannot inherit the kingdom of God, nor does the perishable inherit the imperishable" (v. 50). Our perishable, sin-prone bodies are not suitable for eternity. They must be exchanged for imperishable, glorified bodies like Christ's resurrection body (Philippians 3:20–21).

Correcting Misunderstandings (2 Thessalonians 2:1–12)

Paul wrote 2 Thessalonians to correct misunderstandings about the Day of the Lord and the timing of the Rapture. Apparently, false teachers were claiming that the Thessalonians had missed the Rapture and were now in the Tribulation. Paul refutes this error by reminding them of the events that must take place before the Day of the Lord (the Tribulation) can begin.

Paul writes, "Now concerning the coming of our Lord Jesus Christ and our being gathered together to him" (2 Thessalonians 2:1). The phrases "coming" (*parousia*) and "being gathered together" (*episynagoge*) are technical terms for the Rapture and the resurrection and translation of believers. So Paul is clearly talking about the Rapture in this passage.

He goes on to say that the Day of the Lord cannot come until two things happen: (1) the apostasy (the final rebellion against God) and (2) the revelation of the man of sin (the Antichrist) (v. 3). But he explains that the man of sin cannot be revealed until "he who now restrains ... is out of the way" (v. 7). Most Bible scholars believe this Restrainer is the Holy Spirit working through the Church to hold back the full force of lawlessness. Once the Church is removed via the Rapture, that restraining influence will be gone, and the Antichrist will be revealed.

The Blessed Hope (Titus 2:13)
Paul refers to the Rapture as "waiting for our blessed hope, the appearing of the glory of our great God and Savior Jesus Christ" (Titus 2:13). Notice that the appearing of Christ here is a "blessed hope," not a dreadful or frightening event. For the believer in Christ, the Rapture is a joyful anticipation and expectation.

Other New Testament Passages

Other New Testament writers also mention the Rapture, though not in as much detail as Paul.

Patience Until Jesus Comes (James 5:7–9)
James encourages suffering believers to "be patient, therefore, brothers, until the coming of the Lord.... for the coming of the Lord is at hand" (James 5:7–8). The word for "coming" here again is *parousia*, which we've seen used for the Rapture. James compares

the Lord's coming to a farmer waiting for the precious fruit of harvest—it requires patience but will happen soon.

Setting Our Hope (1 Peter 1:13)

In 1 Peter 1:13, Peter exhorts believers in Christ to "set your hope fully on the grace that will be brought to you at the revelation of Jesus Christ." (This "revelation" (*apokalypsis*) likely refers to the unveiling of Christ at the Rapture. It is a message of grace and hope, not fear or condemnation.

Becoming Like Him (1 John 2:28–3:3)

The apostle John also speaks of the hope of Christ's appearing and the transformation that will take place in believers. He says,

> Beloved, we are God's children now, and what we will be has not yet appeared; but we know that when he appears we shall be like him, because we shall see him as he is. And everyone who thus hopes in him purifies himself as he is pure (1 John 3:2–3).

The prospect of seeing Christ and being made like Him at the Rapture should motivate us to live holy lives now.

Living in Light of the Rapture

From Old Testament types to Jesus' teachings to Paul's epistles, a clear picture of the Rapture emerges.

God's plan has always been to deliver His people from the coming wrath by catching them up to be with Him in Heaven. What an amazing promise and Blessed Hope!

But it's not just a doctrine to be studied; it's also a truth to be lived out. If we really believe Christ could come at any moment to take us home, it should radically impact how we live. It should give us an eternal perspective, a sense of urgency, and a desire to please Him in all we do. Like the five wise virgins in Jesus' parable (Matthew 25:1–13), we should be ready and watching for our Bridegroom's return.

With this biblical foundation for the Rapture firmly in place, we now turn our attention to the signs that this long-awaited event is near. In the next chapters, we will explore the general signs of Christ's coming as well as the specific indicators in society, culture, technology, Israel, and the Middle East that the stage is now set for the Rapture. The prophetic puzzle pieces are rapidly falling into place, telling us that Jesus is coming soon.

5

General Signs the Rapture Is Near

In the previous chapters, we defined the Rapture and distinguished it from the Second Coming, addressed common objections to the doctrine, examined the various views on the timing of the Rapture in relation to the Tribulation, and explored the biblical foundation for this glorious event in both the Old and New Testaments. With this groundwork laid, we now turn our attention to the general signs that indicate the Rapture is drawing near.

While the Rapture is an imminent event that could occur at any moment, Scripture does provide insights into the characteristics and conditions that will mark the time leading up to Christ's return. As we examine these signs, it is important to remember that they are not a checklist of prerequisites that must be fulfilled before the Rapture can occur. Rather, they serve as indicators that we are living in the general season of the Lord's return, and should therefore live with a sense of urgency and expectancy.

Convergence of Signs

One of the most compelling pieces of evidence that we are living in the last days is the unprecedented convergence of *multiple* signs. Jesus spoke of this convergence in His Olivet Discourse, in which He outlined the signs that would characterize the time before His return, such as false messiahs, wars, famines, earthquakes, and persecution (Matthew 24:4–14). While many of these signs have occurred individually throughout history, what makes our day unique is the fact that we are witnessing them all converging and increasing in frequency and intensity simultaneously, like birth pains before delivery (Matthew 24:8).

The apostle Paul also warned of the perilous times that would come in the last days, describing a society marked by godlessness, moral decay, and a love for pleasure rather than God (2 Timothy 3:1–5). The book of Revelation speaks of global turmoil, cosmic disturbances, and the rise of a one-world government and religion during the Tribulation period (Revelation chapters 6–18). As we survey our world today, we see the stage being set for these prophetic events to unfold.

Israel: The Super Sign

We will address Israel more fully in Chapter 7. But perhaps the most significant sign that we are living in the last days is the restoration of Israel as a nation. The Old Testament prophets foretold a time when God would regather His scattered people from the nations and reestablish them in their homeland (Ezekiel 36:24; 37:21; Isaiah 11:11–12; Amos 9:14–15). This began to be fulfilled in the late 19th and early 20th centuries with the Zionist movement and waves of Jewish immigration to Palestine, culminating in the rebirth of Israel as a nation on May 14, 1948.

The fact that Israel is once again a nation, possessing Jerusalem (Luke 21:24), and facing mounting hostility from the surrounding nations, tells us that the prophetic clock is ticking and the Rapture is drawing near.

Rise of Globalism

Another significant sign of the last days is the rise of globalism and the increasing push for a one-world government. The book of Daniel speaks of a coming world empire that will dominate the earth in the End Times (Daniel chapters 2, 7), and Revelation describes a global government, economy, and religion under the rule of the Antichrist (Revelation chapters 13, 17–18). For centuries, the idea of a one-world system seemed impossible. But today, we are witnessing the stage being set for just such a scenario.

Through organizations like the United Nations, World Bank, International Monetary Fund, and World Economic Forum, there is an increasing centralization of power and a push for global governance. Advances in technology, transportation, and communication have made the world more interconnected than ever before. The COVID-19 pandemic also accelerated the trend toward globalism, with world leaders calling for a "Great Reset" and a new global order to address the crisis. While the ultimate fulfillment of these prophecies awaits the Tribulation period, the increasing moves toward globalism in our day are setting the stage for the Antichrist's rise to power.

Increase of Natural Disasters and Pandemics

Jesus said that one of the signs of the End Times would be an increase in "famines and earthquakes in various places" (Matthew 24:7). Some versions, such as the KJV and NKJV include "pestilences" in this verse. While natural disasters and disease outbreaks have occurred throughout history, there seems to be an uptick in both frequency and intensity in recent years. Earthquakes, hurricanes, tsunamis, and wildfires are becoming more prevalent and destructive. Famines are on the rise globally, with the United Nations warning that the world is facing the worst food crisis in 50 years.[1]

Pandemics could well be the pestilences Jesus warned would come in the last days. While not necessarily the specific plagues mentioned in Revelation, worldwide diseases expose the vulnerability of our global systems and the potential for chaos. As the world grows more interconnected, the possibility of rapid, global spread of disease increases. These "birth pains" are a sobering reminder that the Lord's return is drawing near.

Decline of America

While not explicitly mentioned in Bible prophecy, many believers see the decline of the United States as a significant sign of the End Times. For the past century, America has been a superpower and a force for good in the world, using its influence to promote freedom, human rights, and the spread of the gospel. It has also been a staunch ally of Israel. But in recent years, we have witnessed a disturbing moral and spiritual decline in America.

The foundations of faith, family, and freedom that once made America great are being increasingly abandoned and attacked. The sanctity of life, biblical marriage, and religious liberty are under constant assault. Socialists and globalists are seeking to undermine America's sovereignty and transform it into a secular, progressive nation. Many believe that the Rapture of the Church will leave America weakened and vulnerable, hastening its collapse and paving the way for the rise of a global government. While we cannot say with certainty how this will play out, the trajectory of America's decline is certainly a cause for concern and a potential sign of the last days.

Apostasy and Deception in the Church

The Bible warns that the last days will be marked by a falling away from the truth within the Church. Jesus said that false christs and false prophets would arise and deceive many (Matthew 24:4–5, 11, 24). Paul warned of a "great falling away" (apostasy) that would precede the revealing of the Antichrist (2 Thessalonians 2:3). He also said that in the last days, people would not endure sound doctrine but would heap up teachers to suit their own passions, turning away from the truth (2 Timothy 4:3–4).

Sadly, we see these prophecies fulfilled before our eyes. Many churches and denominations that once preached the gospel and upheld biblical truth are now compromising with the world and embracing liberal theology, universalism, syncretism, and moral relativism. False teachers are peddling a watered-down, seeker-friendly message that tickles the ears but denies the power of godliness. Doctrines of demons are leading many astray. The fact that deception and apostasy are increasing, even within the Church, is a clear sign that we are in the last days.

Rise of the Surveillance State and Push for Transhumanism

The development of technology is another significant sign that we are living in the last days. The book of Daniel says that in the time of the end, "Many shall run to and fro, and knowledge shall increase"

(Daniel 12:4). We certainly see an unprecedented explosion of travel and knowledge in our day. But technological advancements are also paving the way for the totalitarian surveillance state and the merging of man and machine that we see in Revelation 13.

Artificial intelligence, facial recognition, biometric scanning, GPS tracking, and social media monitoring are making it easier than ever for the government to monitor and control its citizens. The COVID-19 pandemic only accelerated this trend, with the push for contact tracing, vaccine passports, and digital IDs. At the same time, transhumanist philosophies are gaining traction, with the goal of using technology to enhance and evolve the human body and mind. Microchip implants, brain-computer interfaces, gene editing, and life extension technologies are blurring the lines between man and machine. All of this is setting the stage for the Mark of the Beast system, where people will be required to take a mark on their right hand or forehead to buy, sell, or participate in society (Revelation 13:16–18).

Explosion of Deception, Conspiracy Theories, and Fake News

Another sign that we are living in the last days is the prevalence of deception and the inability to discern truth from lies. Jesus warned that false christs and false prophets would arise and perform great signs and wonders to lead astray, if possible, even the elect

(Matthew 24:24). Paul said that in the last days, people would be deceived by

> "the activity of Satan with all power and false signs and wonders, and with all wicked deception" (2 Thessalonians 2:9–10).

In our day, we see an explosion of conspiracy theories, fake news, deepfakes, and disinformation campaigns. With the rise of social media and alternative news sources, it is becoming increasingly difficult to know what is true and what is false. The mainstream media, once trusted as a source of objective journalism, has become blatantly biased and partisan. Political and cultural leaders manipulate and divide people. The fact that deception is so rampant and truth is so elusive is a clear sign that we are in the last days.

Persecution of Christians

Finally, one of the most sobering signs that we are living in the last days is the increase in persecution of Christians around the world. Jesus warned His disciples that they would be hated and persecuted for His name's sake (Matthew 10:22; 24:9; John 15:18–21). He said that in the last days, people would deliver believers up to tribulation and put them to death (Matthew 24:9).

According to Open Doors' World Watch List 2024, "More than 365m [million] Christians suffer high levels of persecution and discrimination for their faith."[2]

In countries like North Korea, Afghanistan, Somalia, and Libya, Christians face the daily threat of violence, imprisonment, and even death for following Jesus. In the West, Christians are increasingly being marginalized, ridiculed, and censored for holding to biblical values on issues like marriage, sexuality, and the sanctity of life. While persecution has always been a reality for the Church, the fact that it is increasing and intensifying in our day is a clear sign that we are in the last days and that the Lord's return is near.

As we look at these and other signs of the times, we must remember that they are not a cause for fear or despair but rather a call to hope and readiness. The Bible tells us that when we see these things beginning to happen, we should look up and lift up our heads because our redemption is drawing near (Luke 21:28). The convergence of signs in our day is a reminder that the Rapture is imminent.

In the next chapter, we will examine some of the specific societal and cultural signs that are pointing to the soon return of Christ. From the breakdown of the family to the rise of the LGBTQ+ agenda to the war on truth and reality itself, we will see how our world is aligning with the prophetic warnings of Scripture. As the darkness grows even dimmer, may we be found shining brightly as lights in this world, holding fast to the Word of life, until the day of Christ's appearing (Philippians 2:15–16).

6

Specific Societal and Cultural Signs

In the preceding chapters, we laid the foundation for understanding the Rapture and some of the general signs that point to the nearness of this glorious event. We now turn our attention to the specific societal and cultural indicators that we are living in the shadow of the Rapture.

Toxic Moral and Spiritual Climate of the Last Days

One of the clearest signs that we are living in the last days is the toxic moral and spiritual climate that the Bible warns will characterize the period before the return of Christ. In 2 Timothy, Paul paints a disturbing portrait of the prevalent attitudes and behaviors of this time:

> But understand this, that in the last days there will come times of difficulty. For people will be lovers of self, lovers of money, proud, arrogant, abusive, disobedient to their parents, ungrateful, unholy, heartless, unappeasable, slanderous, without self-control,

brutal, not loving good, treacherous, reckless, swollen with conceit, lovers of pleasure rather than lovers of God, having the appearance of godliness, but denying its power. Avoid such people (2 Timothy 3:1–5).

This passage reads like a commentary on our contemporary culture. Everywhere we look, we see the exaltation of self, the obsession with wealth and pleasure, the celebration of pride and arrogance, the normalization of slander and incivility, the loss of self-control and basic decency, and the utter disregard for God and His truth. The apostle Peter echoed this warning, foretelling a time when scoffers would mock the promise of Christ's return and the reality of coming judgment (2 Peter 3:3–4).

We addressed this in the previous chapter, but the toxic moral climate of the last days has also invaded the Church. Jesus warned about what would happen in the days before His return:

> "And then many will fall away and betray one another and hate one another. And many false prophets will arise and lead many astray. And because lawlessness will be increased, the love of many will grow cold" (Matthew 24:10–12).

Sadly, we are living in a day when atheists, skeptics, and even worse, some professing Christians, routinely ridicule the idea of the Rapture and the prophetic truths of God's Word. This is yet another indication that we are living in the last days.

Many professing Christians are adopting the values and behaviors of the world rather than standing firm on the authority of Scripture. This tragedy is unfolding before our eyes, as entire denominations and movements within Christianity abandon biblical orthodoxy and embrace progressive ideologies that contradict the clear teachings of Scripture. Doctrinal compromise, moral relativism, and even outright heresy are rampant in the Church today, leading many astray and setting the stage for the great apostasy that will precede the Rapture (2 Thessalonians 2:3).

At the same time, we are witnessing an explosion of cults, false religions, and pseudo-Christian movements that claim to represent the truth but deny the fundamental tenets of the gospel. This departure from biblical truth is often coupled with a fascination with pagan spirituality, mysticism, and even the occult. Paul warned about the last days:

> Now the Spirit expressly says that in later times some will depart from the faith by devoting themselves to deceitful spirits and teachings of demons (1 Timothy 4:1).

The mainstreaming of witchcraft, astrology, and Eastern spiritual practices in our day is a disturbing fulfillment of this prophecy.

Breakdown of the Family and Assault on God's Design

Another specific sign of the last days is the breakdown of the traditional family unit and the all-out assault on God's design for marriage, sexuality, and gender. In Romans 1:18–32, Paul describes the downward spiral of a society that has rejected God, exchanging the truth for a lie, and embracing homosexuality and sexual perversion as a result.

While this has been true to some degree in every generation since the Fall, we see an unprecedented celebration and institutionalization of sinful behaviors and lifestyles in our day. The LGBTQ+ agenda has gone mainstream, with same-sex marriage now accepted under the law of the land, transgenderism and gender fluidity being taught to young children, and "Pride" paraded down Main Street as the ultimate virtue. Those who hold to the biblical view of marriage and sexuality are increasingly marginalized, vilified, and even criminalized in the public square.

At the same time, God's design for the family is under attack from every direction. Divorce, cohabitation, out-of-wedlock births, and the redefinition of marriage have led to a society where the nuclear family is no longer the norm. Children are growing up in homes without a mother or father, or even with multiple parents of the same sex. The chaos and confusion wrought by these realities are incalculable, leading to a generation that is unmoored from God's truth and ripe for deception.

Escalation of Lawlessness, Violence, and Depravity

Jesus also warned that the last days would resemble the days of Noah, when the earth was filled with violence and corruption (Genesis 6:11–13; Matthew 24:37–39). Tragically, we live in a day when lawlessness, violence, and depravity are the norm in many parts of the world.

From the rise of terrorism and the threat of nuclear war to the epidemic of mass shootings and the scourge of human trafficking, the disregard for human life and basic morality is staggering. Pornography, substance abuse, and every form of sexual immorality run rampant, enslaving and destroying lives on a massive scale. The occult, Satanism, and even the sexualization of children are being normalized and celebrated in popular culture.

All of this points to a world that is descending into utter depravity and ripening for divine judgment. Physical desire and indulgence of carnal appetites are almost worshipped in contemporary society, with those who produce explicit sexual content and advocate for unconventional relationships acting as the purveyors of these new "sacred" values. Immorality and depravity have become accepted norms within our cultural landscape, which many view as an ominous harbinger that we are reaching an existential crossroads.

All Signs Point to Jesus' Return

As we look at specific societal and cultural signs of the last days—the toxic moral and spiritual climate, the breakdown of the family, and the assault on God's design—it becomes clear that we are living in a truly unprecedented time in human history. Never before have we seen such a convergence of prophetic signs, all pointing to the soon return of Jesus Christ.

It's important for us to emphasize that while these signs are alarming and even distressing, they are not a cause for fear or despair for the believer. In fact, Jesus told us that when we see these things beginning to happen, we should look up and lift up our heads, because our redemption is drawing near (Luke 21:28). The darker it gets, the brighter our hope shines. The faster the prophetic dominoes fall, the closer we are to the Rapture and our glorious reunion with Christ. At the same time, these signs should fill us with a sense of urgency to reach the lost with the gospel, knowing that the time is short and the stakes are eternal.

In the next chapter, we will zoom in on some of the specific developments related to Israel and the Middle East that are setting the stage for the fulfillment of end-times prophecy. The super sign of Israel's rebirth as a nation is the prophetic clock that is ticking down to the Rapture and the Tribulation period, and understanding what the Bible says about the centrality of Israel in the last days is crucial for discerning the times in which we live. You won't want to miss this vital part of the prophetic puzzle.

7

Developments Involving Israel and the Middle East

We now turn our attention to the pivotal role that Israel and the Middle East play in the unfolding of end-times prophecy.

Miraculous Rebirth of Israel

As we mentioned earlier, perhaps the most significant sign that we are living in the last days is the miraculous rebirth of the nation of Israel. The Old Testament prophets foretold that in the last days, God would bring the Jewish people back to their ancient homeland after centuries of exile and dispersion (Isaiah 11:11–12; Jeremiah 16:14–15; Ezekiel 36:24–28; Amos 9:14–15). This regathering began to be fulfilled in the late 19th and early 20th centuries with the Zionist movement and waves of Jewish immigration to Palestine.

On May 14, 1948, the impossible happened: the State of Israel was reborn as a nation in a single day, just as Isaiah prophesied (Isaiah 66:8). This was an unprecedented event in human history. For the first time in nearly 1,900 years, the Jewish people had a homeland of their own. The Jews' regathering back to their ancient land after centuries of dispersion is a testament to God's faithfulness and a clear sign that we are living in the final generation before Christ's return (Matthew 24:32–34).

Jerusalem: The Epicenter of End-Times Events

Not only have the Jewish people been regathered to their ancient homeland, but Jerusalem is once again the capital of a reborn Israel. This too is a fulfillment of Bible prophecy and an indication that we are living in the last days. When the Jewish state declared its independence in 1948, Jordan occupied the eastern sector of Jerusalem, including the Temple Mount and Western Wall. For 19 years, the Jews were cut off from their holiest site.

But in the miraculous Six-Day War of 1967, Israel recaptured biblical Judea and Samaria (the so-called West Bank) along with the Golan Heights, the Gaza Strip, and the Sinai Peninsula. Most importantly, they liberated the Old City and reunited Jerusalem under Jewish sovereignty for the first time in nearly two millennia. This was a hugely significant prophetic milestone, fulfilling Jesus' prophecy that Jerusalem would be "trampled underfoot by the Gentiles, until the times of the Gentiles are fulfilled" (Luke 21:24).

Today, Jerusalem has become the focal point of global conflict, just as the Bible predicted. Zechariah 12:2–3 foretells that in the last days, Jerusalem will become "a cup of staggering" (drunkenness) and "a heavy stone" for all nations. The world's obsessive attempts to divide Jerusalem and take it away from Israel are creating increasing tension and hostility, setting the stage for the final battles that will usher in the return of Christ and the arrival of the Antichrist.

Preparations for the Third Temple

Not only have the Jewish people been regathered to their land and Jerusalem recaptured, but preparations to rebuild the Temple are also well underway. The Bible indicates that the Temple will be standing during the Tribulation period, as the Antichrist will desecrate it and declare himself to be God (Matthew 24:15; 2 Thessalonians 2:3–4; Revelation 11:1–2).

In recent years, several Jewish organizations have been established for the sole purpose of rebuilding the Temple. The Temple Institute in Jerusalem (www.templeinstitute.org) has recreated the sacred vessels, garments, and furnishings needed for Temple worship, and they are actively training priests to serve. Unblemished heifers, which are necessary for the purification of the Temple site, have recently been sent to Israel from Texas, creating great excitement among those eager to see the Temple rebuilt.

All the pieces are now in place for the reconstruction of the Third Temple. The fact that plans are being made and preparations undertaken is a powerful sign that we are fast approaching the end of the Church Age and the beginning of the Tribulation period.

Rise of the Gog-Magog Coalition

Another significant development in recent years is the alignment of nations that the Bible says will come against Israel in the last days. In Ezekiel chapters 38–39, we read of a future war in which a coalition of nations, led by Russia and including Iran, Turkey, Libya, Sudan, and others, will launch a massive invasion of Israel. For centuries, it seemed impossible that these nations would ever form an alliance, let alone attack Israel together.

But today, we see this very scenario unfolding before our eyes. Russia and Iran have become close allies, united by their hostility toward Israel and the West. Turkey, which was once a friend of Israel, has become increasingly belligerent under the leadership of President Recep Tayyip Erdoğan. All three of these nations now have a military presence in Syria, right on Israel's northern border.

Iran recently launched an air assault on Israel on April 13, 2024. Although Israel and its allies such as the US, Britain, and France mostly neutralized the attack, for the first time Iranian leaders showed their willingness to carry out a direct attack on Israel. At the same time, Iran has been feverishly pursuing nuclear weapons, and its leaders regularly threaten to wipe Israel off the map. The prophesied alliance that will one day invade Israel is taking shape in our day, just as Ezekiel foretold over 2,500 years ago. This is yet another powerful sign that we are living in the shadow of the Tribulation and the Lord's return.

Alignment of Nations and Mounting Threats Against Israel

In addition to the specific nations mentioned in Ezekiel chapters 38–39, we also see a broader alignment of nations against Israel in recent months. Following Hamas's attack on Israel in October 2023 and Israel's military response in Gaza, the tiny Jewish state is now surrounded by enemies on all sides who are united in their desire to see it destroyed. Some Bible scholars see Psalm 83 as a prophetic text that speaks of a confederacy of nations:

> They say, "Come, let us wipe them out as a nation;
> let the name of Israel be remembered no
> more!" (v. 4).

Today, Israel faces threats from Hamas in Gaza, Hezbollah in Lebanon, and hostile nations like Iran and Syria. Much of the Arab world is united in its opposition to Israel's existence, and the international community routinely condemns Israel for defending itself against terrorist attacks.

At the same time, the worldwide rise of antisemitism is further evidence that we are living in the last days. The irrational hatred of the Jewish people is reaching levels not seen since the days of Nazi Germany, and attacks against Jews are becoming increasingly common in Europe and even in the United States.

Significance of Israel's Rebirth for the Church

As we look at all these developments surrounding Israel and the Middle East, it's important to understand their significance for the Church. The facts that Israel exists as a nation today and that Jerusalem is once again the capital of the Jewish state are powerful confirmations of the faithfulness of God's Word.

The Lord made an everlasting covenant with Abraham, Isaac, and Jacob, promising to give their descendants the land of Canaan as an eternal possession (Genesis 17:7–8). He also promised He would one day regather His people from the nations and bring them back to their land (Ezekiel 36:24). The fact that these promises are being fulfilled in our day is a testament to the trustworthiness of the Bible.

But the regathering of Israel is also significant because it is setting the stage for the fulfillment of end-times prophecy. The Bible tells us that in the last days, the Antichrist will rise to power and confirm a seven-year covenant with Israel (Daniel 9:27).

This covenant will allow the Jews to rebuild their Temple and reinstitute the sacrificial system.

However, halfway through the seven-year period, the Antichrist will break his covenant and desecrate the Temple, declaring himself to be God (2 Thessalonians 2:3–4). This event, known as the "Abomination of Desolation," will mark the beginning of the Great Tribulation, a time of unparalleled suffering and persecution for the Jewish people (Matthew 24:15–21).

As believers in Jesus Christ today, we will not be present on the earth during this time of trouble. The Rapture will take place before the Tribulation begins, and we will be caught up to meet the Lord in the air (1 Thessalonians 4:16–17). However, the fact that we see the stage being set for these events to unfold should fill us with a sense of urgency to share the gospel with those who are lost.

Importance of Standing with Israel

In light of all that is happening in Israel and the Middle East, it is crucial that we as believers stand with the Jewish people and support the nation of Israel. The Bible tells us that God will bless those who bless Israel and curse those who curse her (Genesis 12:3). As Christians, we have a biblical mandate to pray for the peace of Jerusalem (Psalm 122:6) and to comfort the Jewish people (Isaiah 40:1–2).

This does not mean that we blindly support every action taken by the Israeli government or that we condone any wrongdoing on their part. But it does mean that we recognize Israel's right to exist as a nation and that we stand with her against the forces of evil that seek to destroy her people.

In a world that is increasingly hostile toward Israel and the Jewish people, it is important that we as believers are a voice of support and encouragement. We must speak out against antisemitism in all its forms and stand in solidarity with our Jewish friends and neighbors. And we must always remember that the Jewish people are still God's chosen people, beloved for the sake of their forefathers (Romans 11:28).

Ongoing Implications

As we look at the developments surrounding Israel and the Middle East, it is a clear sign that we are living in the last days. The regathering of the Jewish people to their ancient homeland, the reunification of Jerusalem under Israeli control, the preparations to rebuild the Temple, and the alignment of nations against Israel are all signs that the stage is being set for the fulfillment of Bible prophecy.

However, these developments should not cause us to fear or despair. Rather, they should fill us with hope and expectancy. The fact that we see these things coming to pass is a powerful reminder that God is in control and that His plan for the ages is unfolding just as He said it would.

As we move forward, let us keep our eyes fixed on Israel and the Middle East, knowing that what happens there will have profound implications for the entire world. Continually pray for the peace of Jerusalem and for the salvation of the Jewish people.

———————

In the next chapter, we will explore another exciting aspect of the Rapture: the astronomical signs in the heavens that point to the nearness of Christ's return. Just as the wise men were once guided by a star to the birthplace of the Messiah, so too are there signs in the sun, moon, and stars that herald His soon return. As we study these celestial wonders and their prophetic significance, we will see even more clearly that the stage is set for the greatest event in human history.

8

Astronomical Signs in the Heavens

We have been looking at the general signs indicating we are living in the last days before Christ's return, such as the convergence of prophetic signs, the restoration of Israel, the rise of globalism, and the increasing apostasy and moral decay in the world and within the Church. Now we turn our attention to another fascinating category of signs that appear in the heavens above us.

Throughout the Bible, God emphasizes the importance of signs in the sun, moon, and stars. In Genesis 1:14, He declares that the lights in the expanse of the heavens are to serve as "signs and for seasons, and for days and years." The Hebrew word for "seasons" here is *mow'edim*, which means "appointed times" and is used in Leviticus 23 to describe the seven Feasts of Israel. So from the beginning, God intended the celestial bodies to be markers of prophetic events on His calendar.

Jesus affirmed that "there will be signs in sun and moon and stars" that would indicate the season of His return (Luke 21:25–28). He said that when we see these signs begin to happen, we should look up and lift up our heads, because our redemption is drawing near. Other prophetic passages also speak of astronomical disturbances that will mark the onset of the Day of the Lord and the return of Christ (Joel 2:30–31; Acts 2:19–20; Revelation 6:12–14).

So what are some of these significant signs God seems to be declaring in the heavens in our day? Let's examine a few of the most compelling ones.

The Blood Moons of 2014–2015

One of the most talked about astronomical signs in recent years was the rare phenomenon known as a tetrad of blood moons. A blood moon is a total lunar eclipse in which the moon takes on a reddish color. It's a striking fulfillment of the prophecies that the moon will be turned to blood before the great and terrible Day of the Lord (Joel 2:31).

While blood moons are not extremely rare, what is remarkable is when a series of four blood moons occurred in a row on the biblical feast days of Passover and Tabernacles. This happened in 2014–2015, and it has only occurred three other times in the last 500 years—each time coinciding with a major event in Jewish history.

In **1493–1494,** a tetrad of blood moons on the feast days occurred just after the Spanish Inquisition and expulsion of the Jews from Spain. In **1949–1950,** it happened again as the nation of Israel was being reborn. And in **1967–1968,** another tetrad of feast day blood moons occurred during the Six-Day War when Israel recaptured Jerusalem.

So what was the significance of the **2014–2015** blood moons? It's impossible to say for certain, but they seem to be another heavenly sign that God is up to something major in His prophetic plan, especially related to Israel. It's as if He is trying to get our attention that the end is near and that the Rapture of the Church and the following Tribulation period are rapidly approaching.

The Revelation 12 Sign

On September 23, 2017, an extremely rare astronomical alignment occurred that many believe was a literal fulfillment of the "great sign" described in Revelation 12:1–2. In this passage, the apostle John sees a vision of a woman clothed with the sun, with the moon under her feet, and a crown of twelve stars on her head. He then witnesses a great red dragon that seeks to devour the woman's child as soon as it is born.

Many Bible prophecy experts believe this imagery represents the nation of Israel (the woman) and the Messiah (the male child). The twelve stars represent the twelve tribes of Israel. The red dragon symbolizes Satan and his age-long attempt to prevent the coming of the promised Seed of the woman who would crush his head (Genesis 3:15).

In an extraordinary celestial display, this sign seemed to appear in the skies on September 23,

2017. On that date, the sun was in the constellation Virgo (the virgin), with the moon under her feet. Above her head were three planets—Mercury, Mars, and Venus—along with the nine stars of the constellation Leo, making a "crown" of twelve stars. The planet Jupiter had been in the "womb" area of Virgo for nine months (the length of a human pregnancy), and it moved out of Virgo on that day as if being "born."

The precision and rarity of this alignment is staggering. It had not occurred before and will not occur again for thousands of years. What could be the prophetic significance? Again, we must be cautious about making dogmatic assertions, but it is certainly a sign that got the attention of prophecy students worldwide. It seems to be another indication that God is signaling the nearness of the end-times events, including the Rapture, the Tribulation, and the Second Coming of Christ.

Other Significant Celestial Signs

The blood moons and Revelation 12 sign are by far the most compelling astronomical signs that have appeared in recent years. But several other interesting celestial events are also worth mentioning:

- The "Bethlehem Star" conjunction of Jupiter and Venus on June 30, 2015, that some believe mirrored the famed Star of Bethlehem the Magi saw at Christ's first coming.

- The total solar eclipse that traversed the United States on August 21, 2017—a rare event that had not occurred since 1918. Another total solar eclipse crossed the US on April 8, 2024, marking an "X" over the nation.

- A unique series of three "supermoons" in late 2016 in which the moon appeared up to 30 percent brighter and 14 percent larger than normal.

- Hundreds of reports of increased fireball and meteor activity, strange sounds from the sky, and other unusual sights and signs.

While we stress again that we must avoid sensationalism and date setting around these events, their increased frequency and intensity seems to be another indicator that we are living in the last days before Christ's return. The signs are piling up at a faster pace, as if God is shouting from the heavens that the King is coming soon!

The Purpose of Astronomical Signs

So what is the purpose of these signs in the sun, moon, and stars? Is God just trying to put on a celestial fireworks show to wow us? No, He has a much deeper purpose in mind. The signs are meant to be a prophetic wake-up call to get our attention and cause us to look up.

Jesus said that when these signs begin to happen, we should "straighten up and raise your heads, because your redemption is drawing near" (Luke 21:28). He compares them to a fig tree putting forth leaves, indicating that summer is near. In the same way, the astronomical signs are indicators that the Rapture and the Day of the Lord are at the door.

The apostle Peter gives us further insight into how we should respond to the prophetic signs. He writes:

> But the day of the Lord will come like a thief, and then the heavens will pass away with a roar, and the heavenly bodies will be burned up and dissolved, and the earth and the works that are done on it will be exposed.
>
> Since all these things are thus to be dissolved, what sort of people ought you to be in lives of holiness and godliness, waiting for and hastening the coming of the day of God, because of which the heavens will be set on fire and dissolved, and the heavenly bodies will melt as they burn! (2 Peter 3:10–12).

Peter is saying since the Rapture can happen at any moment and the destruction of the Day of the Lord will follow, we should be living holy and godly lives as we watch for Christ's appearing. Like the wise virgins in Jesus' parable (Matthew 25:1–13), we must keep our lamps full of the oil of the Spirit and our wicks trimmed in expectation of the Bridegroom's sudden arrival.

The heavenly disturbances are a cosmic alarm clock going off to rouse a sleeping Church. They are

God's billboards advertising the imminent return of His Son. Just as the wise men were watching the skies and spotted the star that led them to the Messiah's first appearing, we should be scanning the heavens for the signs of Jesus coming again.

How Do We Respond?

So how should we live in light of the astronomical signs of the end? Here are a few practical exhortations:

1. **Look up and lift your head** in hopeful expectation. The celestial signs are heralds of our coming redemption and reunion with Christ. While they may bring distress and perplexity to the world, they should bring joy and anticipation to the bride of Christ!

2. **Wake up and clean up.** It's time to shake off spiritual slumber and be watchful and ready for our Lord's appearing. Let's root out any moral compromise or besetting sin in our lives and pursue holiness with greater passion.

3. **Stock up on the oil of intimacy with God.** Like the wise virgins, we need to be continually filled with the Spirit through abiding in the Word, waiting on the Lord, and praying without ceasing.

4. **Evangelize the lost with urgency.** The signs indicate that the day of salvation is almost

over and the Day of the Lord is at hand. We must redeem the time and reach the lost while there is still opportunity.

5. **Encourage one another with the hope of the Rapture.** As the world gets darker, the "blessed hope" of the Rapture shines brighter. Comfort one another with the truth of Christ's soon return for His bride.

Just as the spectacular signs in the heavens stir our hearts, our imagination is invited to picture the next great event on God's prophetic calendar—that glorious moment when the Church is caught up to meet the Lord in the air! At the Rapture, a stunning heavenly reunion awaits every blood-bought child of God. At last, the bride will see her Bridegroom face to face! In the next chapter, we will explore what it will be like to experience the Rapture and meet Jesus in the air. Get ready for your heart to soar as we anticipate this climax for which all creation longs!

9

Meeting Jesus in the Air

In the preceding chapters, we laid a solid foundation for understanding the Rapture and looked at the many signs that point to the nearness of Christ's return for His Church. All of these converging signs tell us that the Rapture is rapidly approaching. With each passing day, we draw closer to that glorious moment when the trumpet will sound, the dead in Christ will rise, and we will be caught up to meet the Lord in the air!

The Promise of Our Heavenly Reunion

As we contemplate the Rapture, one aspect that should thrill our hearts above all others is the precious promise of our face-to-face meeting with Jesus. Throughout Scripture, we find this "blessed hope" woven like a golden thread, filling us with joyful anticipation. In the Upper Room on the night before His death, Jesus comforted His disciples with these words:

> "Let not your hearts be troubled. Believe in God; believe also in me. In my Father's house are many

rooms. If it were not so, would I have told you that I go to prepare a place for you? And if I go and prepare a place for you, I will come again and will take you to myself, that where I am you may be also" (John 14:1–3).

As we noted earlier, in this passage, Jesus assures us that He is preparing a heavenly home for us and that He will come again to receive us unto Himself. The Greek word translated "receive" means to 'take to oneself' and was used of a bridegroom coming for his bride. Just as the Jewish bridegroom would go to prepare a place for his bride and then return to take her to his father's house, so Jesus, our Heavenly Bridegroom, is coming to take us, His bride, to His Father's house in Heaven. What a beautiful picture of the intimate reunion that awaits us!

The apostle Paul gives further details about this glorious event in 1 Thessalonians:

> For the Lord himself will descend from heaven with a cry of command, with the voice of an archangel, and with the sound of the trumpet of God. And the dead in Christ will rise first. Then we who are alive, who are left, will be caught up together with them in the clouds to meet the Lord in the air, and so we will always be with the Lord (1 Thessalonians 4:16–17).

Back in Chapter 4, we broke down the specific details Paul tells us about the Rapture, but we will remind you of those here:

1. The Return of Christ

Notice it is "the Lord himself" who will descend from Heaven. This is not some intermediary or representative but Jesus Christ in all His resurrected glory and majesty. The same Jesus who died for our sins, rose on the third day, and ascended to the right hand of the Father is the One who will personally come for us at the Rapture.

2. The Accompanying Sounds

When Christ descends, He will come "with a cry of command, with the voice of an archangel, and with the sound of the trumpet of God" (v. 16). The cry of command or shout could be the Lord Himself breaking through the barrier between Heaven and earth with a cry of triumph and a summons for His saints. The voice of the archangel (perhaps Michael, the great prince and protector of Israel) will herald the resurrection of the righteous. And the trumpet of God will be the final trumpet that signals the end of the Church Age and the beginning of the Day of the Lord.

3. The Resurrection of the Dead in Christ

"The dead in Christ will rise first." Paul is referring to all Church-Age believers who have died up to the time of the Rapture. In an instant, the bodies of millions of saints will be resurrected from their graves, gloriously transformed into immortal, incorruptible bodies like Christ's resurrection body. These believers have been with the Lord in spirit since the moment of death (2 Corinthians 5:8), but now they will be reunited with their perfected physical bodies. What an incredible display of God's resurrection power!

4. The Rapture of Living Believers

"Then we who are alive and remain shall be caught up together with them in the clouds to meet the Lord in the air." Immediately after the dead in Christ rise, living believers will be instantaneously changed or translated "in a moment, in the twinkling of an eye" (1 Corinthians 15:51–52). Without experiencing death, we will be caught up—raptured—to meet the Lord.

As we said previously, the Greek word for "caught up" is *harpazō*, which means 'to snatch or seize suddenly, to carry off by force.' It has the idea of a quick, irresistible act of catching away. This same word is used of Philip being supernaturally transported from the desert to Azotus (Acts 8:39–40). So in a split second, the Rapture will forcefully snatch us from earth to the clouds above. One moment we'll be going about our daily lives; the next we'll be in the presence of Jesus, experiencing the most radical change imaginable!

5. Meeting in the Air

The Rapture will unite the resurrected dead and the transformed living "to meet the Lord in the air." The word translated "meet" was used in Greek to refer to a welcoming party going out to meet a visiting dignitary and then accompanying him back to the place from which they came. So Christ will come to the realm between Heaven and earth to claim His bride, and we will meet Him in the air. He will then escort us back with Him to Heaven for the Marriage Supper of the Lamb (Revelation 19:6–9).

This meeting in the air is an important detail that distinguishes the Rapture from the Second Coming. At the Rapture, Jesus comes for His saints and takes them from earth to Heaven. But at the Second Coming, He will come with His saints from Heaven to earth to rule and reign in His Millennial Kingdom (Zechariah 14:4–5; Revelation 19:14). As we noted earlier, the many differences between the Rapture and the Second Coming make it clear that they are separate events.

6. Forever With the Lord

The ultimate purpose of the Rapture is not just a momentary meeting in the air but to be with Jesus forever: "And so we shall always be with the Lord." From the time we rise to meet Him, we will never again be separated from His presence. Through the Tribulation period, the Millennial Kingdom, and on into the eternal state, we will be with Christ, enjoying unbroken fellowship with Him and reigning by His side. This has been the deepest longing of our hearts, and it will finally be fully realized.

Can you imagine what that first face-to-face encounter with Jesus will be like? To see your Savior, your Redeemer, your Bridegroom in all His glory and majesty? To feel His nail-pierced hands embrace you, to hear His voice welcome you, to gaze into His eyes of infinite love? What unspeakable joy, what holy awe, what heavenly bliss will flood our souls!

Emotions of the Raptured

It's impossible to fully fathom the roller coaster of emotions we will experience in that split second of the Rapture. Instant elation, as the weight of sin, sickness, and sorrow falls away and we're catapulted into the presence of pure holiness. Immediate relief, as the burdens we've carried and the pain we've endured are swallowed up in total victory. Complete awe, as our mortal minds are overwhelmed by the unveiled glory of God. Perfect peace, as we're enveloped in the love of Christ that has been the anchor of our souls.

There may be a momentary sense of disorientation, as we suddenly cross the space-time threshold into the eternal realm. But that will quickly give way to unrestrained euphoria over our new glorified state. No more aches, no more aging, no more battling the flesh. Only unlimited joy, undiminished strength, and unbroken worship before the Throne of God.

From Rapture to Reward

For us, the Rapture will be a thrilling exit from this fallen world and an entrance into glory. But it is not the end of our journey. After we meet the Lord in the air, we will remain in Heaven with Him for a period of time while the earth below experiences the unprecedented horrors of the Tribulation. During that interlude, we will stand before the Judgment Seat of Christ to receive our eternal rewards, and we will celebrate our union with the Lamb at the Marriage Supper.

Then, at the appointed time, we will accompany the Lord Jesus as He returns in power and great glory to defeat His enemies, bind Satan, and establish His Millennial Kingdom on earth. As His redeemed people and His glorious bride, we will share in His triumphal return and reign with Him for a thousand years.

So the Rapture is not the consummation but the inception of an eternal adventure in which we will explore the endless vistas of God's grace and glory in the ages to come. Words fail to describe all that awaits us on the other side of the Rapture!

We Can Hardly Wait

As we have seen, the Rapture is not just an end-times event to be debated and charted on a prophetic timeline. It is also a precious promise to be cherished, a "blessed hope" to be anticipated. We should not only be looking for the Rapture but also longing for the One who is coming to take us home. The signs tell us it could happen at any moment. Jesus is at the very gates!

Does the imminent prospect of meeting Christ face-to-face thrill your heart and purify your life (1 John 3:2–3)? Or does it find you entangled in the cares of this world and the deceitfulness of riches? The Rapture will be the ultimate dividing line between the prepared and the unprepared. In the twinkling of an eye, the watching will be taken, and the worldly will be left.

We pray that you will be found ready and waiting, with your lamp burning and your heart yearning for that glorious moment when the Bridegroom comes. Fix your eyes on the eastern sky, eagerly scan the horizon for the sign of His appearing. Lift up your head in joyful expectation, knowing that your redemption is drawing near. Live each day in light of eternity, occupied with your Master's business until He returns.

With the Rapture, we will bid a fond farewell to this fallen world and experience our great homegoing to Heaven. But as glorious as that will be, it is only the first phase of the eternal ecstasy that awaits us. In the next chapter, we'll explore what happens immediately after the Rapture, as we receive our resurrection bodies and our Savior's reward.

Resurrection and Transformation

With each passing day, we draw closer to that glorious moment when the trumpet will sound, the dead in Christ will rise, and we will be caught up to meet the Lord in the air! But there is another incredible aspect of the Rapture that we must explore—the miraculous transformation that will happen to us in that instant.

Not only will we be caught up to Heaven, but we will also be changed in the twinkling of an eye from mortal to immortal, from perishable to imperishable. This resurrection and glorification of the saints is a core aspect of the Rapture that should thrill our hearts and fill us with hope. Let's dive into what the Bible says about this amazing metamorphosis that awaits us.

The Promise of Resurrection

The bodily resurrection of believers is a fundamental tenet of the Christian faith, foretold in the Old Testament (Job 19:25–27; Psalm 16:9–11; Isaiah 26:19;

Daniel 12:2) and confirmed in the New Testament. Jesus Himself spoke of a coming hour when "all who are in the tombs will hear his voice and come out" (John 5:28–29). He declared, "I am the resurrection and the life. Whoever believes in me, though he die, yet shall he live, and everyone who lives and believes in me shall never die" (John 11:25–26). Jesus' own resurrection is the firstfruits and guarantee of the future resurrection of His people (1 Corinthians 15:20–23). Because He conquered the grave, we know we too will rise.

The apostle Paul provides the most detailed revelation of resurrection in 1 Corinthians 15. He explains that the resurrection body will be imperishable, glorious, powerful, and spiritual (vv. 42–44). It will bear continuity with our present body, but be radically transformed—from natural to supernatural, from earthly to heavenly, from mortal to immortal (vv. 45–49). This is the ultimate victory over death that God has promised (vv. 54–57).

The apostle John assures us that when Christ appears, "we shall be like Him" (1 John 3:2). So Jesus' glorified resurrection body is the prototype of the new body we will receive. After His resurrection, Jesus was recognizable, yet His appearance was different enough that Mary and the disciples didn't immediately know Him (John 20:14–16; 21:4, 12). His body was physical—He could be touched, and He ate food (Luke 24:39–43). Yet He also could appear and disappear at will and seemingly walk through solid surfaces (Luke 24:31, 36; John 20:19, 26). So our resurrection bodies will be tangible and recognizable, yet supernatural in capacities and no longer bound by the limitations of our current bodies.

The Rapture: Resurrection and Transformation

The resurrection of the righteous dead of the Church Age will occur in the same instant as the transformation of living believers at the Rapture. Paul describes this mystery in 1 Corinthians:

> Behold! I tell you a mystery. We shall not all sleep, but we shall all be changed, in a moment, in the twinkling of an eye, at the last trumpet. For the trumpet will sound, and the dead will be raised imperishable, and we shall be changed. For this perishable body must put on the imperishable, and this mortal body must put on immortality (1 Corinthians 15:51–53).

Paul had previously explained the sequence of this event to the Thessalonians:

> For the Lord himself will descend from heaven with a cry of command, with the voice of an archangel, and with the sound of the trumpet of God. And the dead in Christ will rise first. Then we who are alive, who are left, will be caught up together with them in the clouds to meet the Lord in the air, and so we will always be with the Lord (1 Thessalonians 4:16–17).

So at the moment of the Rapture, two distinct but simultaneous miracles will occur: the resurrection of deceased Church-Age saints and the glorification of living believers.

The Dead in Christ Rise

All believers who have died from the Day of Pentecost until the Rapture—regardless of when, where, or how—will have their bodies instantly resurrected, made immortal and incorruptible (Philippians 3:20–21). No matter how long a body has been in the grave or what state of decay it has undergone, God will reconstitute it in perfection in the blink of an eye. Every Christian grave on earth will be emptied as the dead in Christ rise first to meet the Lord.

This fulfills God's pledge of 2 Corinthians 4:14:

> Knowing that he who raised the Lord Jesus will raise us also with Jesus and bring us with you into his presence.

Death cannot separate us from God's love or His power to resurrect (Romans 8:38–39). Those who have died in faith are not left out of the Rapture but have priority in the order of events.

Believers Caught Up and Changed

Immediately after the dead are raised, living believers will be transformed and caught up. Paul writes that we "will be caught up together with them in the clouds to meet the Lord in the air, and so we will always be with the Lord" (1 Thessalonians 4:17). The transformation of living saints will happen "in a moment, in the twinkling of an eye" (1 Corinthians 15:52). The Greek word for "moment" is *atomos*, meaning something that can't be divided—an indivisible instant. The "twinkling of an eye" speaks of the time it takes for light to flash off the surface of the eye. In other words, it will be instantaneous—a split-second change from one state to another.

In that nanosecond, "this perishable body must put on the imperishable, and this mortal body must put on immortality" (1 Corinthians 15:53). Our decaying, sin-prone, death-doomed bodies will be renovated from the inside out with unending, indestructible life. We will go from perishable to imperishable without passing through death. Like Enoch who was taken to Heaven without dying (Genesis 5:24; Hebrews 11:5), we will trade mortality for immortality in a flash as we are caught up to glory.

Nature of the Resurrection Body

What will our resurrection bodies be like? The Bible gives some intriguing insights. First, they will be like Christ's glorious body. The apostle Paul states,

> But our citizenship is in heaven, and from it we await a Savior, the Lord Jesus Christ, who will transform our lowly body to be like his glorious body, by the power that enables him even to subject all things to himself (Philippians 3:20–21).

So Jesus' resurrection body is the model and proto-type of the body we will receive.

Here are some key characteristics of our resurrection bodies according to 1 Corinthians 15:

Imperishable and immortal (vv. 42, 52–54)—They will never age, decay, deteriorate, die, or experience the effects of sin's curse. They are forever liberated from death and corruption.

Glorious (v. 43)—Dazzling, radiant, and beautiful, free from any defect, deficiency, or imperfection. They will reflect the perfection and splendor of Christ Himself.

Powerful (v. 4 3)—Possessing abilities, strength, and energy beyond our current mortal limitations—fit for reigning with Christ and serving Him eternally. No more weakness, fatigue, or frailty.

Spiritual (v. 44)—Not ethereal or immaterial but totally subject to and animated by the Spirit as our natural bodies are animated by the soul. Perfectly designed for life in God's eternal Kingdom.

Heavenly (vv. 47–49)—No longer fitted for earthly existence but tailor-made for life in Heaven. Bearing the image of the resurrected and glorified Christ.

These resurrection bodies will be real, physical bodies (Luke 24:39) yet supernaturally transformed and no longer bound by natural laws. We will be able to eat (Luke 24:41–43), be embraced (Matthew 28:9), and communicate (John 21:15). Yet we will also be able to appear and vanish at will (Luke 24:31, 36), pass through solid objects (John 20:19, 26), defy gravity (Acts 1:9–10), and travel effortlessly through space and dimensions.

Our new bodies will be liberated from all sin's effects, including sickness, pain, sorrow, decay, and death (Revelation 21:4). There will be no more cancer, heart disease, diabetes, arthritis, depression, disabilities, or defects. We will experience perfect health and wholeness in a form that never wears out.

Additionally, our new bodies will be recognizable—not a different person but the best possible version of us. The disciples recognized Jesus after His resurrection (John 20:16, 20; 21:12). At the Transfiguration, the disciples knew Moses and Elijah though they had never seen them before (Matthew 17:3–4). So we will know our loved ones and they will know us—but without any of sin's flaws or failures.

Our resurrection bodies will be ageless, timeless, and eternal—forever beyond the reach of sin and the Fall and under the glorious liberty of the children of God (Romans 8:21, 23). They will be perfectly fashioned for worship, service, and enjoyment of God in the New Heavens and New Earth. With an unhindered capacity for fellowship with the Lord and one another, we will not be confined to a single space but will reign and rule with Him over all creation.

Practical Implications and Motivation

The promise of the resurrection and our coming bodily transformation has tremendous implications for how we live and minister today. It should impact us in at least three ways:

1. An Eternal Perspective and Hope

Knowing that these weak, perishable, mortal bodies will soon be exchanged for powerful, imperishable, glorious bodies should lift our eyes above the trials and tribulations of this world. When the struggles of our decaying flesh weigh us down, we can look forward to the coming liberation of the children of God (Romans 8:18–25).

As Paul reminds us,

> For this light momentary affliction is preparing for us an eternal weight of glory beyond all comparison, as we look not to the things that are seen but to the things that are unseen. For the things that are seen are transient, but the things that are unseen are eternal (2 Corinthians 4:17–18).

The sufferings and groanings we experience now are temporary. One day soon all pain, death, crying, and sorrow will pass away as we are clothed with life and immortality (Revelation 21:4; 2 Corinthians 5:4). So we do not lose heart, for though our outward man is perishing, our inward man is being renewed day by day (2 Corinthians 4:16). We eagerly await the redemption of our bodies at the Rapture (Romans 8:23).

2. Motivation for Holy Living

The fact that we will be changed in an instant should motivate us to live holy and godly lives. Our current bodies are not our own; they have been bought with the price of Christ's blood (1 Corinthians 6:19–20). We are to glorify God in our bodies now, knowing one day they will be transformed to glorify Him for eternity.

As Paul exhorts in Romans 12:1, in view of God's mercies, we are to present our bodies as a living sacrifice, holy and acceptable to Him. We're to flee sexual immorality and impurity, knowing that our bodies are temples of the Holy Spirit (1 Corinthians 6:18–20). Instead of gratifying the sinful desires of the flesh, we're to walk in purity, self-control, and sober watchfulness as we await our blessed hope (Titus 2:11–14; 1 Thessalonians 5:1–11).

The Rapture and resurrection should also stir us to be abounding in the work of the Lord, knowing that nothing we do for Him is in vain (1 Corinthians 15:58). As long as we have breath, we are to occupy till He comes, investing our time and talents to further His Kingdom (Luke 19:13). For one day soon we will stand before Him to give an account and receive a just reward for the deeds done in the body (2 Corinthians 5:10).

3. Comfort for Those Who Grieve

The truth of the Rapture and resurrection also provides immense comfort for those believers who have lost loved ones in Christ. It assures us that the separation is only temporary. Though we grieve, we do not grieve as those who have no hope (1 Thessalonians 4:13). For since we believe that Jesus died and rose again, we know that God will bring with Him those who sleep in Jesus (v.14).

When the Rapture occurs, we will be reunited forever with beloved family and friends in the Lord (1 Thessalonians 4:17–18). What a delight it will be on that day to embrace without end the ones we love! Every heartache and pain of separation will be swallowed up in the joy of eternal fellowship. Tears of grief will be transformed to songs of celebration as we praise God together around the Throne.

The knowledge that deceased saints are with the Lord (2 Corinthians 5:8) and will be raised first in the Rapture gives the assurance that they will not miss out on the glory to be revealed. Their bodies will be resurrected in power and splendor and caught up a split second before the living. So we can entrust them to their faithful Savior, confident that not even death can separate them from Him (Romans 8:38–39).

The Climax of Our Salvation Story

The Rapture and resurrection of the Church is a glorious promise that should thrill our hearts and shape our priorities. In the twinkling of an eye, we will be changed—from death to life, from corruption to incorruption, from mortal to immortal, from weakness to power, from humiliation to glorification. These lowly bodies ravaged by sin will be instantly reshaped into conformity with Christ's glorious body.

Everything that has been placed under the curse—sickness, sorrow, pain, decay, and death—will be eradicated in this cosmic metamorphosis. We will be made completely whole, radiantly perfect, and ready for life in the eternal state with our King. No more wrestling with the flesh, no more battling temptation, no more groaning over our fallenness. Only total freedom, complete joy, and unbroken fellowship with our Redeemer.

The resurrection and transformation of our bodies is the climax of our salvation story—the full realization of God's purpose to transform us into the image of His Son (Romans 8:29). It is the fulfillment of the pledge of redemption made to us by the Holy Spirit (Ephesians 1:13–14; 4:30). He who began this good work of conforming us to Christ will complete it at the Rapture (Philippians 1:6).

When the burdens of this body of death weigh heavily on you, look up! Your frail tent will soon be replaced with a glorious, heavenly building. Your perishable flesh will burst forth in power and put on the imperishable. Your mortal frame will be swallowed up by immortality!

As glorious as the Rapture and resurrection will be, it is still not the end but only the beginning of a series of momentous prophetic events. Immediately after we rise to meet the Lord in the air, we will be ushered into His presence to stand before the

Judgment Seat of Christ and participate in the Marriage Supper of the Lamb. In the next chapter, we'll explore what Scripture reveals about these incredible proceedings in Heaven as the earth below enters the darkest period in its history. Get ready to have your works evaluated and your devotion to Christ celebrated!

The Judgment Seat of Christ and Marriage Supper of the Lamb

What happens immediately after the dead in Christ rise first and we who are alive are caught up together with them to meet the Lord in the air? The Rapture is not the end of the story but rather the gateway to an entirely new series of glorious prophetic events and experiences that await the redeemed of God. As we pass through the clouds and transition to the heavenly realm, we will enter into two incredible proceedings: the Judgment Seat of Christ, where our works will be evaluated, and the Marriage Supper of the Lamb, where we will celebrate our eternal union with our Heavenly Bridegroom.

So let's take a few moments to consider what the Scriptures reveal about these next chapters in the great unfolding story of redemption.

The Bema Seat Evaluation

When Paul was transported to the third Heaven, perhaps during his Damascus road encounter with

Jesus, he had visions and revelations of the Lord that were so spectacular he could hardly describe them (2 Corinthians 12:2–4). Among the things he learned and later taught was the truth about a coming judgment for believers that would not determine salvation but assign or withhold eternal rewards based on how we lived our lives after conversion.

Paul wrote about this in two key passages:

> For we must all appear before the judgment seat of Christ, so that each one may receive what is due for what he has done in the body, whether good or evil (2 Corinthians 5:10).

> Why do you pass judgment on your brother? Or you, why do you despise your brother? For we will all stand before the judgment seat of God; for it is written,
>
> > "As I live, says the Lord, every knee shall bow to me, and every tongue shall confess to God."
>
> So then each of us will give an account of himself to God (Romans 14:10–12).

The Greek word for "judgment seat" here is *bema,* which referred to a raised platform in ancient amphitheaters and athletic contests where victors would go to receive their awards, crowns, and accolades after being evaluated for their performance. Paul is depicting this scene as a type of what believers will experience after the Rapture. It will not be a judgment of sin, since that has already been paid for by Christ at the cross, but rather a time of examination, assessment, and commendation before the Lord.

But make no mistake—this will be a solemn and sobering event, not to be taken lightly. The quality and motives of our lives, not just the outer appearance, will be laid bare before the penetrating gaze of God Himself. Paul writes,

> Each one's work will become manifest, for the Day will disclose it, because it will be revealed by fire, and the fire will test what sort of work each one has done. If the work that anyone has built on the foundation survives, he will receive a reward. If anyone's work is burned up, he will suffer loss, though he himself will be saved, but only as through fire (1 Corinthians 3:13–15).

The Evaluative Fire

Paul uses the metaphor of fire to describe this time of intense scrutiny. Every believer's works—habits, priorities, choices, investments, ministry, witness, and relationships—will be put through the purifying fire of God's perfect holiness. Those things done in the power of the Spirit and for the glory of Christ (the gold, silver, precious stones) will prove genuine and endure for eternity. But those things done in the power of the flesh, for selfish ambition or human approval (the wood, hay, stubble) will be incinerated on the spot and returned to ashes.

Think of the earthly accomplishments, accolades, and works that men and women often live for and seek to build their legacy on—wealth, status, academic credentials, business empires, military conquests, artistic achievements, civic honors, political influence, and social prominence. At the Judgment Seat, any and all such accomplishments pursued for the sake of self-aggrandizement instead of the glory of Christ will instantly go up in smoke, leaving nothing behind.

Even if all our worldly pursuits, in both the sacred and secular realms, end up being fanned to ashes in His presence, our salvation remains intact and secure. But what a tragic waste of the time, talent, and potential God entrusted to us if it cannot withstand the flame that penetrates to the core motivation of every thought, word, and deed. What could be more heartbreaking than to see our entire life's "work" reduced to smoldering ruins?

So this is no casual evaluation or lighthearted awards banquet. It is the ultimate accountability moment for those who claim Jesus Christ as Lord and Savior—a time to see every aspect of our lives examined, exposed, and evaluated for eternity. Everything will be revealed—the good, the bad, and the ugly. All our public successes and secret sins. All our hidden motives and works done behind the scenes. The real reasons we did and said what we did and said.

These sobering thoughts should fill us with a sense of godly fear and a desire to prepare our hearts now for that day. Like the prophet Malachi says,

But who can endure the day of his coming, and who can stand when he appears? For he is like a refiner's fire and like fullers' soap (Malachi 3:2).

When we stand before our Maker and Judge, may we be found faithful and true, having built with eternal materials for His glory alone.

The Bestowing of Rewards

The good news is that while the fire strips away every vestige of hypocrisy and self-promotion, it doesn't consume those genuine works that stem from a pure love for and devotion to Christ. Whatever is of true eternal value—every righteous deed, every obedient choice, every hidden act of sacrificial service, and every soul won for the Kingdom—will prove indestructible and become the basis for receiving eternal rewards.

One of the main rewards mentioned in Scripture is the bestowal of crowns, which we will then humbly cast at the feet of Jesus in worship. Paul spoke of the imperishable crown for those who mastered their fleshly passions (1 Corinthians 9:25). Jesus promised a crown of life to those who persevere under trial (Revelation 2:10). James wrote of a crown of glory for faithful elders (James 1:12). Peter described the unfading crown of glory awaiting those who shepherd God's flock (1 Peter 5:1–4). And Paul anticipated the crown of righteousness for those who love the Lord's appearing (2 Timothy 4:8).

Think about it—in this glorious setting, having already been made perfect and glorified just moments before at the Rapture, we will actually have the chance to present back to Christ the righteous accomplishments He empowered and grace He supplied for the works we did for Him. What rejoicing there will be to hear "Well done, good and faithful servant" on those deeds that truly counted for His Kingdom!

But the ultimate reward that will outshine any crowns or accolades will be the smile of our Master's approval and commendation that we lived as disciples whose aim was to please and glorify Him alone. As John wrote, "We know that when he appears we shall be like him, because we shall see him as he is" (1 John 3:2). To gaze unshielded into the eyes of our Savior and hear Him validate the lives we lived for His glory—that will greater than any other earthly or heavenly prize.

The Judgment Seat is not something to be feared by those walking in purity and faithfulness. Rather, it should inspire us to build our lives on the things that will last forever, with eternal values and heavenly treasures. That's why Paul exhorted the Corinthians to "be steadfast, immovable, always abounding in the work of the Lord, knowing that in the Lord your labor is not in vain" (1 Corinthians 15:58). This isn't a meaningless life we're living. Every sacrifice and service given to Christ has infinite significance and an everlasting reward awaiting us in Heaven.

The Marriage Supper of the Lamb

As monumental as the Judgment Seat will be, it is but the opening act to one of the grandest and most magnificent celebrations the universe will ever know: the Marriage Supper of the Lamb! This breathtaking occasion is described in Revelation 19:

> Then I heard what seemed to be the voice of a great multitude, like the roar of many waters and like the sound of mighty peals of thunder, crying out,
>
> > "Hallelujah!
> > For the Lord our God
> >   the Almighty reigns.
> > Let us rejoice and exult
> >   and give him the glory,
> > for the marriage of the Lamb has come,
> >   and his Bride has made herself ready;
> > it was granted her to clothe herself
> >   with fine linen, bright and pure"—
> > for the fine linen is the righteous deeds of the saints.
>
> And the angel said to me, "Write this: Blessed are those who are invited to the marriage supper of the Lamb." And he said to me, "These are the true words of God" (Revelation 19:6–9).

From Genesis to Revelation, God portrays His relationship with His covenant people in terms of a spiritual marriage. In the Old Testament, Israel was depicted as the wife of Yahweh, with whom He had a binding covenant. But in the New Covenant, the Church has become the virgin bride of Christ, betrothed, and waiting for the Marriage of the Lamb to consummate the eternal union.

That grand bridal celebration is about to commence! The imagery invokes the ancient Jewish wedding tradition, where a husband would go away to prepare a place for His bride while she got ready, gathering and creating her wedding hope chest. Then at a predetermined time but often an unexpected hour, the groom would return. His shout would summon the bride, she would quickly adorn herself, and they would be united forever in marriage, followed by a seven-day wedding feast.

The parallels are striking. At His first coming, our Bridegroom Christ paid the infinite purchase price to redeem and secure His bride by His sacrificial death on the cross (1 Corinthians 6:20). He then "went to prepare a place" for us by ascending back to His Father's heavenly house to get everything ready for the wedding (John 14:2–3).

Meanwhile, we as His bride have been getting ourselves ready during this Church Age, washing our robes in His blood and adorning ourselves with the righteous deeds and fruit of sanctification He produces in us (Ephesians 5:25–27). The moment of the Rapture will correspond to the cry of the Groom as He comes to receive us to Himself so that where He is, we may be also. And then the Wedding Feast in Heaven can begin!

The Bible doesn't specify how long the Marriage Supper will last, but it will most certainly be an extended and lavish celebration. We are told that the bride, the Church, has made herself ready and been given the garment of fine linen, representing the righteous acts of the saints. Can you picture the radiant bride of Christ finally being presented to the universe in all her blood-bought beauty, clothed in splendor and arrayed in full readiness for the "big day"? This is the consummation of the ages when Christ takes His spotless bride unto Himself forever! How all of Heaven will erupt in praise to see the sacred vows sealed between God's eternal Son and His beloved betrothed ones.

Believers, behold your Bridegroom face to face! Angels, stand in awestruck wonder at redeeming love displayed! The armies of God's redeemed from every nation, tribe, and tongue merging their voices in the unending anthem: "Worthy is the Lamb who was slain!" This will be the wedding party of all wedding parties, an eternal delight of intimate fellowship, pure and unrestrained joy in the presence of the Lamb, and unbridled exaltation of the Bridegroom!

The location where these festivities take place could be the New Jerusalem, that palatial inheritance Christ has been preparing for His bride to share together (John 14:2–3; Revelation 21:2, 9–27). It seems fitting that the consummation of this marriage will occur where the Lamb and His wife will dwell in the sinless, sorrow-free paradise of eternity. With the vibrant river of life flowing from the throne and trees of life yielding fresh fruit each month, what better Garden than God's eternal capital for the long-awaited Wedding Feast to commence?

Some suggest the Marriage Supper will transpire throughout the duration of the seven-year Tribulation on earth, while others contend it's a separate, shorter event leading into the long Millennial Reign of Christ on earth. Regardless of the length or setting, one thing seems certain: when believers meet their Bridegroom face-to-face at last, inexpressible delight and intimate communion will be ours forevermore!

In the ancient world, weddings and wedding feasts were seen as the highest occasions of festivity, the most joyous celebrations imaginable. Garments and jewelry were made ready. The finest foods were prepared. Songs and music filled the air. Friends and family gathered from all around to share in the occasion. All of life's energies and resources were poured into throwing the party of all parties to commemorate the establishment of a new family lineage.

Can you imagine what great eternal rejoicing and revelry will fill the courts of Heaven when the Son of God marries His redeemed people? All of redemptive history has been building toward this grand union and occasion! As mind-boggling as it may seem, our eternal destiny is not just to be forgiven sinners destined for Heaven but also to become the cherished bride of the Bridegroom King who loved us and gave Himself for us (Ephesians 5:25).

We can barely understand the intimacy and ecstatic union that awaits us at the Marriage Supper, where we will forever fellowship with our Beloved and gaze upon His unveiled glory! Jesus Himself promised to drink the fruit of the vine anew at that banquet (Matthew 26:29). What could be greater than partaking of the cup from His hand in that celebration of limitless love and everlasting communion?

As joyous and splendid as weddings are on earth, they are but the faintest echo of the unimagined bliss to come at this Marriage Supper of the Lamb. Our grandest earthly feasts and festivities could never compare to the lavish fare and unrestrained merriment that awaits. Every earthly love story, no matter how romantic, has been but a faded signpost pointing to the delight and eternal joy between Christ and His redeemed bride on that day!

So prepare your soul's affections. Make yourself ready in holiness and devotion, for what has been promised is beyond your greatest dreams. Don't settle for lesser loves. Our Bridegroom is coming! And the joys of that Wedding Day and Supper will forever outshine every earthly experience of intimacy and every earthly banquet.

> What no eye has seen, nor ear heard,
> nor the heart of man imagined,
> what God has prepared for those who love him
> (1 Corinthians 2:9)

Shaping Our Priorities and Our Passions

The Judgment Seat of Christ and the Marriage Supper of the Lamb are two events that remind us of the importance of living with an eternal perspective and in a state of readiness for the coming of our Bridegroom King. These future realities should shape the priorities and passions of our earthly lives, motivating us to build our hopes and dreams on Heaven's realities.

At the Judgment Seat, the secret motives and true intents behind all our words, deeds, and choices will finally be revealed for what they are. Every shred of hypocrisy, selfishness, and self-promotion will go up in flames, while every work done in faithful obedience and devotion to Christ will win His praise and reward.

At the Marriage Supper, we will enter into the eternal union our souls have longed for since the moment we first believed. As the spotless bride of Christ, we will at last see Him face to face in all His beauty and be ushered into the never-ending marriage feast of joy unspeakable and intimate communion with our Beloved Savior.

Let this knowledge shape your life. Very soon we will stand before the Lord to have our lives weighed in the balances of His holiness. Give your heart's affection and obedience to the One alone who is preparing us as His bride to share in the coming eternal feast. He is coming for us quickly; the cry of our returning Bridegroom could go forth at any moment.

This should be our focus and desire: to be found worthy of our calling and spotless in His sight, with no cause for shame but every reason to "straighten up and raise your heads, because your redemption is drawing near" (Luke 21:28).

But what about those who are left behind on earth after the Rapture? What happens to them when the judgments of the Tribulation period finally begin to unfold? In the next chapter, we'll take an in-depth look at the shockwaves that will reverberate across the world after millions of people have suddenly disappeared. We'll examine the rise of the Antichrist and the chaos he will bring, the persecution of those who become believers during the Tribulation, and the catastrophic judgments that will rain down from Heaven as God's wrath is poured out on a Christ-rejecting world.

For those left behind, the Rapture will not be some joyous celebration but the beginning of the most terrifying time in human history—a period aptly called the Great Tribulation (Matthew 24:21). Sudden destruction will come upon the indifferent and the scoffers like labor pains upon a pregnant woman (1 Thessalonians 5:3). God will send a powerful delusion and harden the hearts of those who chose not to believe the truth (2 Thessalonians 2:11–12). The only hope will be to embrace Christ, endure to the end, and refuse to take the Mark of the Beast (Revelation 13:16–18), even if it costs them their lives.

As horrible as the Tribulation will be, it is ultimately an act of mercy from God, a final wake-up call to turn to Him before it's eternally too late. His judgments during this time will be a severe but righteous response to the worldwide rebellion against His authority. The Tribulation is a sobering reminder that God's patience has limits and the stakes for rejecting His Son are infinitely higher than we can ever comprehend.

For believers, the Rapture will usher in our long-awaited deliverance and the celebration of the Wedding Feast with our Bridegroom King. But for those left behind, it will signal the beginning of the darkest period in world history. May the prospect of missing out on the Rapture and being forced to endure the horrors of the Tribulation motivate people everywhere to heed God's call while there is still time. The signs are converging, and the spiritual birth pains are increasing in frequency and intensity— our Groom is coming quickly! As we'll see in the next chapter, being ready for His return is a matter of utmost urgency.

12

The Tribulation and the Antichrist

While the Church is caught up to Heaven in a glorious deliverance, the world left behind will be plunged into its darkest hour: the seven-year Tribulation period. Let's examine what the Bible reveals about this time of unparalleled horror and upheaval on the earth.

Shock and Devastation in the Aftermath

The Rapture will come like a thief in the night, suddenly and without warning (1 Thessalonians 5:2). In an instant, millions of people will vanish from the face of the earth, leaving behind crashed vehicles, crippled services, and devastated families. The ensuing chaos and confusion will be beyond imagination.

Those left behind will grapple for answers to the mass disappearances. Speculation will run rampant, with theories ranging from alien abductions to government conspiracies. But one man will rise from the turmoil with an air of authority, offering explanations and solutions that will deceive the masses.

Rise of the Antichrist's Global Empire

This smooth orator and political genius will be the Antichrist, Satan's false messiah who will exploit the Rapture's aftermath to seize world control. His meteoric rise to power is foreshadowed in Daniel chapters 7–8 and Revelation chapter 13.

With his magnetic personality and miraculous abilities, the Antichrist will present himself as a savior, establishing a one-world government, economy, and religion. He will make a seven-year covenant with Israel, promising peace and allowing the Jews to rebuild their Temple.

But halfway through the Tribulation, the Antichrist will reveal his true colors. He will betray Israel, declare himself to be God, and demand worldwide worship of his image. This Abomination of Desolation, when he will profane Jerusalem's Temple and blaspheme God, will mark the onset of the Great Tribulation—the most severe judgments yet unleashed.

The Persecution of the Tribulation Saints

As the Antichrist implements his demonic agenda, a remnant of believers will emerge. These saints may be new converts since the time of the Rapture. Empowered by the Holy Spirit, they will boldly refuse to worship the Beast or take his mark.

As a result, they will face unthinkable persecution from the Antichrist and his followers. Believers will be hunted, imprisoned, tortured, and martyred for their faith. As Revelation 6:9–11 and 13:7 reveal, a countless multitude will pay the ultimate price for choosing Christ over the Antichrist.

Yet these Tribulation saints will be spiritually victorious over the devil:

> And they have conquered him by the blood of the Lamb and by the word of their testimony, for they loved not their lives even unto death (Revelation 12:11).

They will receive white robes and special honor for their sacrifice (Revelation 7:9–17; 20:4).

The Unfolding Judgments and Catastrophes

As the Antichrist's empire tightens its grip on the world, God will begin pouring out His righteous wrath through a series of unparalleled judgments. These progressive calamities are depicted in Revelation as Seven Seals, Seven Trumpets, and Seven Bowls.

The Seal Judgments will bring the Four Horsemen of the Apocalypse: deception, war, famine, and death. A quarter of the world's population will be destroyed under the fourth seal (Revelation 6:7–8).

The Trumpet Judgments will unleash demonic locusts to torment all humanity, meteors to poison the earth's waters, and fire from Heaven to devastate the landscape. Over a third of the planet's ecosystem will be annihilated (Revelation chapters 8–9).

The Bowl Judgments will culminate in a final outpouring of divine wrath, with the earth scorched by fire, the seas turned to blood, the sun supernaturally darkened, and 100-pound hailstones falling from the sky. The Euphrates River will dry up, paving the way for the Battle of Armageddon (Revelation chapter 16).

Throughout the Tribulation, the earth will be pummeled by cosmic disasters, ecological catastrophes, pandemics, and world war. The death toll will be beyond calculation. The Antichrist will be powerless to stop God's vengeance against his satanic empire.

The Final Spiritual Showdown

As the judgments intensify, so will the battle for human souls. The 144,000 sealed Israelites will preach the gospel across the globe (Revelation 7:1–8). The Two Witnesses will proclaim God's truth from Jerusalem for 1,260 days before the Antichrist kills them and displays their bodies as a gruesome trophy (Revelation 11:1–14).

An angel will fly through Heaven, urging mankind to fear God and reject the Beast (Revelation 14:6–7). The Holy Spirit will be poured out in unprecedented measure, as a great multitude from every nation comes to Christ (Joel 2:28–32).

The Tribulation is thus a time of both wrath and mercy, as God simultaneously judges a God-rejecting world and extends grace to all who will repent. It is the ultimate reckoning between the seed of the serpent and the Seed of the woman—the final conflict before Christ's return.

The Church's Glorious Exemption

But we as the Church have nothing to fear from the seven-year reign of the Antichrist. We are not appointed to wrath but to obtain salvation through our Lord Jesus Christ (1 Thessalonians 5:9). We will be kept from the hour of trial coming upon the whole earth (Revelation 3:10).

Instead of facing the Tribulation, we will enjoy the reward seat of Christ and the Marriage Supper of the Lamb in Heaven. We will receive our immortal bodies and reign with Christ as His beloved bride.

The Tribulation should thus motivate us not to shrink back in dread but to reach forward in hope. It should compel us not to cower in fear but to boldly proclaim the gospel while there's still time. As the world grows darker, our "blessed hope" shines brighter.

God's Purposes Fulfilled

In this chapter, we've touched on the horrors of the Tribulation. We've seen the shock and devastation the Rapture will leave in its wake, the Antichrist's satanic rise to power, the unthinkable persecution believers will endure, and the catastrophic judgments that will decimate the earth.

But we've also seen the unprecedented spiritual harvest that will occur as 144,000 sealed Israelites, the Two Witnesses, an angelic evangelist, and the Tribulation saints preach the gospel to every nation before the end.

As dreadful as the Tribulation will be, it serves a divine purpose. It is a final call to repentance for an unbelieving world. It is a purging of a God-rejecting earth before the Millennial Reign of Christ. And it is a reminder to us as believers of the urgent need to reach the lost before it's too late.

In the next chapter, we'll explore the climax of the Tribulation and all of human history: the glorious Second Coming of Christ. No longer the humble Lamb, He will return as the conquering Lion to destroy the Antichrist, bind Satan, and establish His Kingdom on earth. What a breathtaking scene that will be as the King of kings and Lord of lords rides in on a white horse with the armies of Heaven! Get ready for the final countdown to the most majestic moment of the ages.

Second Coming, Millennium, and Eternity

As glorious as the Rapture will be, it is not the end of God's prophetic program. It is the gateway to the darkest period in human history, the seven-year Tribulation, when the Antichrist will rise to power, God's wrath will be poured out on the earth, and believers will face unparalleled persecution. But this time of unprecedented turmoil and suffering will culminate in the most triumphant event in history: the Second Coming of Jesus Christ.

The Glorious Return of the King

Unlike the Rapture, which will be a sudden snatching away of the Church, the Second Coming will be a public, visible event witnessed by the whole world. Revelation 1:7 says,

> Behold, he is coming with the clouds, and every eye will see him, even those who pierced him, and all tribes of the earth will wail on account of him. Even so. Amen.

This is the moment Jesus Himself predicted in Matthew 24:30:

> "Then will appear in heaven the sign of the Son of Man, and then all the tribes of the earth will mourn, and they will see the Son of Man coming on the clouds of heaven with power and great glory."

What a breathtaking sight that will be! Revelation 19:11–16 describes it in vivid detail:

> Then I saw heaven opened, and behold, a white horse! The one sitting on it is called Faithful and True, and in righteousness he judges and makes war. His eyes are like a flame of fire, and on his head are many diadems, and he has a name written that no one knows but himself. He is clothed in a robe dipped in blood, and the name by which he is called is The Word of God. And the armies of heaven, arrayed in fine linen, white and pure, were following him on white horses. From his mouth comes a sharp sword with which to strike down the nations, and he will rule them with a rod of iron. He will tread the winepress of the fury of the wrath of God the Almighty. On his robe and on his thigh he has a name written, King of kings and Lord of lords.

This will not be the meek and mild Jesus of the first coming but the mighty warrior King and righteous Judge. With the armies of Heaven following Him, He will strike down the nations, treading "the winepress of the fury of the wrath of God the

Almighty" (Revelation 19:15). He will destroy the Antichrist and his forces with the brightness of His coming (2 Thessalonians 2:8), casting the Beast and False Prophet into the Lake of Fire (Revelation 19:20). Satan himself will be bound and imprisoned in the Bottomless Pit for a thousand years (Revelation 20:1–3).

The Second Coming will mark the end of the times of the Gentiles and the beginning of the Messianic Age. When Christ's feet touch the Mount of Olives, the mountain will split, creating a great valley (Zechariah 14:4). He will liberate Jerusalem, enter the city through the Eastern Gate, and take His seat on the throne of David. The Deliverer will come out of Zion and turn godlessness away from Jacob (Romans 11:26). The day that Israel has longed for will finally arrive as their Messiah-King comes to establish His Kingdom and reign over the nations.

The Millennial Kingdom

With all opposition vanquished, the curse lifted, and creation restored, King Jesus will inaugurate His thousand-year reign on earth, fulfilling God's covenant promises to Israel. He will rule the world in righteousness from His capital in Jerusalem, and the saints from all ages will reign with Him (Revelation 20:4–6).

The Millennium will be a time of unprecedented peace and prosperity as Christ governs the nations with a rod of iron (Psalm 2:9; Revelation 12:5). War and injustice will cease as the world beats swords into plowshares (Isaiah 2:4) and the knowledge of the Lord covers the earth (Isaiah 11:9). The animal kingdom will return to its Edenic harmony, with the wolf and the lamb grazing together (Isaiah 11:6). The desert will blossom like a rose (Isaiah 35:1), and people will live long, productive lives (Isaiah 65:20–23). The whole earth will be filled with the glory of Christ (Habakkuk 2:14).

During this golden age, Israel will finally enjoy her complete inheritance in the Promised Land. The Jewish people will be regathered from the nations, reunited as one nation under the Messiah's rule (Ezekiel 37:21–28). The Temple will be rebuilt, and memorial sacrifices will be offered as a tribute to Christ's finished work on the cross (Ezekiel chapters 40–48). The feasts will be celebrated and the Sabbath observed (Zechariah 14:16–19). Jerusalem will be the praise of all the earth as the nations stream to Zion to worship the King (Isaiah 2:2–4).

Yet despite the perfect environment and Christ's visible reign, the Millennium will demonstrate that the human heart is still prone to sin. Children born during this age will need to trust Christ to be saved. And when Satan is released at the end of the thousand years, he will find willing subjects to join his rebellion against God (Revelation 20:7–9). But this final insurrection will be short-lived, as fire comes down from Heaven to consume the rebels. The devil will then be cast into the Lake of Fire forever (Revelation 20:10).

The Great White Throne Judgment

Following this climactic event, all the unbelieving dead from all ages will be resurrected to face the Final Judgment before the Great White Throne (Revelation 20:11–15). The books will be opened, and the lost will be judged according to their works. Those whose names are not found written in the Book of Life will be cast into the Lake of Fire, which is the second death—an eternal separation from the goodness and grace of God. This solemn scene reminds us of the urgency of reaching the lost with the gospel while there is still time. Hebrews 9:27 states, "It is appointed for man to die once, and after that comes judgment."

The Eternal State

With sin and death forever vanquished, God will unveil the eternal state: a New Heaven and a New Earth where righteousness dwells (2 Peter 3:13; Revelation 21:1). The New Jerusalem, our eternal home, will descend out of Heaven, radiant with the glory of God (Revelation 21:2, 11). The Father Himself will dwell among us, wiping away every tear from our eyes (Revelation 21:3–4). The Lamb will be our Temple and the Light of the city (Revelation 21:22–23). The River and Tree of Life will nourish and heal the nations (Revelation 22:1–2). Curse and night will be no more (Revelation 22:3, 5).

In this glorious city, we will reign with Christ as kings and priests forever and ever (Revelation 22:5). We will worship, serve, explore, create, and fellowship in ways we can't begin to imagine. Every pleasure will be pure, every relationship whole, and every moment infused with joy inexpressible. Best of all, we will see our Savior's face and be forever with the One who died for us and rose again (Revelation 22:4; 1 Thessalonians 4:17). Eden will be restored and exceeded as God and man dwell together in perfect harmony for all eternity.

This is the consummation of our Blessed Hope! It is the anchor for our souls, the joy set before us, the prize of the upward call of God in Christ Jesus (Hebrews 6:19; 12:2; Philippians 3:14). It is what makes every trial, every persecution, every heartache in this life pale in comparison to the glory that awaits (Romans 8:18; 2 Corinthians 4:17). Indeed,

> "What no eye has seen, nor ear heard,
>   nor the heart of man imagined,
> what God has prepared for those who love him"
>   (1 Corinthians 2:9).

As we have seen throughout this study, the Rapture is not just an arcane point of theology or the pet theory of prophecy buffs. It is the next event on God's prophetic calendar, the "blessed hope" of every blood-bought child of God (Titus 2:13). The signs of the times are shouting that it is near, even at the doors (Matthew 24:33; James 5:8–9). The spirit of Antichrist is growing bolder, the love of many is growing colder, and the fig tree is putting forth its leaves. The birth pangs are increasing, and the stage is being set for the final act. The trumpet is about to sound, and the Bridegroom is ready to descend!

Three Exhortations

So what kind of people are we to be as we await this imminent event (2 Peter 3:10–12)? How then should we live in light of the Rapture happening at any moment, followed by the Tribulation, that Millennium, and the eternal state? Let us close this chapter with three exhortations:

1. **Watch expectantly.** Keep looking up, for your redemption is drawing near (Luke 21:28). Be sober, watchful, and alert, living each day as if it could be the day of His coming (1 Thessalonians 5:6; Revelation 16:15).

2. **Occupy faithfully.** If the Master's return is near, let Him find you doing His business (Luke 19:13). Don't waste your time on frivolous pursuits or your resources on fleeting pleasures. Be a good steward of all God has entrusted to you, investing in that which is eternal (1 Corinthians 3:11–15). Live in the light of the Judgment Seat of Christ (2 Corinthians 5:10) and make it your ambition to please Him (2 Corinthians 5:9). Let your conduct be worthy of the gospel (Philippians 1:27).

3. **Witness urgently.** The time is short, and the day is rapidly approaching when no man can

work (1 Corinthians 7:29; John 9:4). Lift up your eyes and see that the fields are white for harvest (John 4:35). Warn the lost to flee from the wrath to come (1 Thessalonians 1:10) and share with them the Good News of Christ's coming and the salvation He offers.

Becoming Rapture Ready

Throughout the pages of this book, we have explored the profound biblical truth of the Rapture—that glorious moment when Jesus Christ will descend from Heaven, resurrect deceased Church-Age believers, and catch up living saints to meet Him in the air, taking us to the Father's House for all eternity.

We began by clearly defining the Rapture and distinguishing it from the Second Coming. We then tackled some of the common objections and questions surrounding this doctrine, demonstrating that it is firmly rooted in Scripture and has been believed by Christians since the early centuries of the Church.

Next, we examined the various views on the timing of the Rapture in relation to the Tribulation period, laying out a compelling case for the pre-Tribulation position based on a face-value reading of key prophetic biblical passages. To further solidify the biblical foundation for the Rapture, we traced it through the types and shadows of the Old Testament, the teachings of Jesus, and the writings of Paul and the other apostles.

As we surveyed the prophetic landscape, we looked at the many signs indicating that we are living in the last days before Christ's return. From the convergence of general signs like geopolitical turmoil, apostasy, and the rise of globalism, to the specific societal and cultural indicators of the breakdown of morality and the rejection of God's truth, it's clear that the stage is being set for the Rapture and Tribulation.

Israel's miraculous restoration as a nation and the growing alignment of enemies against her are the super sign that the prophetic clock is ticking toward the Rapture and the rise of Antichrist. Even the heavens are declaring the season of His return, as we have witnessed the tetrad of blood moons on Jewish feast days and other significant astronomical signs.

As we contemplated that breathtaking moment when the trumpet sounds and we rise to meet Jesus in the air, we marveled at the glorious transformation that will take place: our mortal, corruptible bodies instantly changed into immortal, incorruptible bodies like our Lord's resurrection body. We will be reunited with resurrected loved ones in Christ and ushered into the presence of our Bridegroom King to enjoy the most intimate union and unbroken fellowship at the Marriage Supper of the Lamb.

While the Church experiences glory and bliss in Heaven, the earth will descend into unprecedented chaos and judgment as the wrath of the Lamb is poured out on a Christ-rejecting world.

We examined the shock waves the Rapture will generate, the meteoric rise of the Antichrist and his demonic empire, the unthinkable persecution of Tribulation believers, and the catastrophic Seal, Trumpet and Bowl Judgments that will decimate the planet.

As dreadful as the Tribulation will be, we took great hope in the unprecedented spiritual harvest that will occur as 144,000 sealed Israelites, the Two Witnesses, an angelic evangelist, and fearless Tribulation saints preach the gospel to every nation before the end.

Finally, we explored the climax of all history—Christ's glorious Second Coming, when He returns in power to vanquish His foes, redeem Israel, and establish His literal thousand-year Kingdom on earth. The curse will be reversed, creation will be restored, and righteousness will reign, "for the earth shall be full of the knowledge of the LORD as the waters cover the sea" (Isaiah 11:9).

After a final uprising by Satan is swiftly crushed, the current universe will melt away in a fervent heat, and God will usher in the New Heavens and New Earth. All things will be made new as He dwells forever with His people in unspeakable beauty, joy, and glory in the eternal state.

Live with Urgency and Expectancy

In light of these stunning realities, how should we then live? The Rapture is not just a doctrine to be debated but also a promise to be anticipated and a truth that should radically reshape our priorities and pursuits. As Romans 13:11–12 exhorts us, we must awaken from spiritual slumber and live with a sense of urgency, casting off the deeds of darkness and putting on the armor of light. The King is coming—perhaps today! We must be about our Father's business, maximizing every moment for His glory.

Pursue Holiness and Purity

The imminent return of Christ should also motivate us to pursue holiness and purity as we prepare to meet our Lord face to face. "And everyone who thus hopes in him purifies himself as he is pure" (1 John 3:3). In a world that is increasingly immersed in darkness, perversion, and godlessness, we are called to be lights on a hill, keeping our conduct honorable and our consciences clean.

Invest in Eternal Rewards

Recognizing that our life is a vapor and that we will soon stand before the Judgment Seat of Christ to give an account should compel us to invest our time, talent, and treasure in that which will endure for eternity. Rather than chasing the fleeting pleasures and possessions of this world, we should seek first His Kingdom, laying up imperishable treasures in Heaven where neither moth nor rust destroys.

Endure Suffering Faithfully

As we await the Rapture, we must be prepared to endure hardship and persecution for the name of Christ. While we are not destined for the wrath of God, we are promised tribulation in this world. But we must not lose heart, for "the sufferings of this present time are not worth comparing with the glory that is to be revealed to us" (Romans 8:18). The hope of the Rapture gives us an eternal perspective to persevere through trials, fixing our eyes on Jesus, "the founder and perfecter of our faith" (Hebrews 12:2).

Look for His Appearing

Above all, the Rapture should create in us an intense longing and holy anticipation for Christ's appearing. Like the Thessalonians, we should be known as those who have turned from idols to serve the living God and to "wait for His Son from heaven" (1 Thessalonians 1:9–10). We are a bride eagerly counting the days until we see our Beloved face to face.

Encourage One Another

Living in the last days can be disorienting and discouraging at times as we see so many falling away from biblical truth. That's why it's crucial that we continue "encouraging one another, and all the more as you see the Day drawing near" (Hebrews 10:25). We need the support and exhortation of like-minded believers to stay strong, steadfast, and focused on Christ.

———————

The Rapture is not a fairy tale; it is the sure promise of Almighty God. While we cannot know the day or hour, we can know with absolute certainty that Jesus is coming *for* us before He comes back *with* us. Knowing what we know about the stunning events that await us should cause us to live with an eternal perspective.

The signs tell us He is at the very gates! It could be at any moment. Let's be found ready and waiting, with our lamps burning and our hearts yearning for His appearing.

Frequently Asked Questions

Q: What is the significance of the Rapture in relation to the Tribulation?
A: We know from Bible prophecy that the Rapture will occur before the Tribulation. First is the Rapture at the beginning of the Tribulation, then the Second Coming at the end of the Tribulation.

Q: What happens to believers at the Rapture versus the Second Coming?
A: At the Rapture, living believers will be caught up to meet Jesus in the air. This is a private event between Jesus and the Church. In contrast, the Second Coming will be a public event where every eye sees Jesus accompanied by the Church that He has wed at the Marriage Supper of the Lamb returning to earth, specifically to Jerusalem.

Q: What is the relationship between the Rapture and the Marriage Supper of the Lamb?
A: Between the Rapture and Second Coming, the Raptured Church will participate in the Marriage

Supper of the Lamb in Heaven. This will occur during the same seven-year period as the Tribulation is happening on earth.

Q: Revelation 13:7 says that the Antichrist had power over the saints. How can this happen if we were raptured?
A: That's not referring to us. The Church is raptured at the beginning of the Tribulation. But there will probably be hundreds of millions of people saved during the Tribulation. There's a Rapture of the Church at the beginning of the Tribulation, but the people who get saved during the Tribulation will join us and Jesus at the end of the Tribulation.

Q: If I question God about where He is during these difficult times, does that mean I won't get raptured?
A: Absolutely not. If you've received Jesus as the Lord of your life, you're saved. Christians have questions, and they go through difficulties. Sometimes they get angry at God, and sometimes they question God. That doesn't mean you're not going up in the Rapture. The most important thing in preparing for the Rapture is knowing Jesus Christ personally. None one is perfect. We're all saved by grace. If you know Him personally, you're going to go up in the Rapture.

Q: Does every ear have to hear the gospel of Jesus Christ before the Rapture can take place?
A: The gospel will be preached by the end of the Tribulation. The gospel is going around the world right now via satellite, radio, internet, and human missionaries, but every tribe, nation, and tongue will hear it before Jesus returns at the Second Coming. That does not mean it has to happen before the Rapture. It might, but it's not required for the Rapture to happen.

Q: I have a bad habit and want to stop. Will my disobedience keep me from the Rapture?
A: The only thing that qualifies you for the Rapture is to know Jesus Christ as your Lord and Savior. If you're a Christian—if you know Jesus personally as your Lord and Savior—then you're going in the Rapture. We're saved by grace and not by works.

Q: I greatly fear the Rapture because some of my family members are not saved. Am I not saved for thinking like this?
A: If you weren't saved, you wouldn't care. The reason you care about your family is because you are saved. When Jesus comes, you're going to go with Him. If they are not saved, they're going to be left behind. Be a good example to your family, pray for your family, and share your faith with them. There's a possibility of them being saved after the Rapture, but the Tribulation will be a severe time. By what

you're doing now, hopefully some of your family will be saved (if not all of them).

Q: If we believe that the Rapture is very near, should we be concerned about politics?
A: We should be preparing for the Rapture and concerned about our culture. As good citizens, we will lose our freedoms if we don't stand up for them. Our responsibility is to focus both on making disciples and standing up for what is right as citizens. Both choices are part of our Christian witness.

Q: What happens if someone is pregnant at the Rapture?
A: All children before they reach the age of accountability and whose parents are believers will be caught up with their parents to be with the Lord. God loves to save households of people.

Q: Why is it called the Second Coming if Jesus actually returns during the Rapture and then again after the Tribulation? Why not call it the third coming?
A: The Second Coming is one event that happens in different phases or stages. The Second Coming is going to happen in two phases: the Rapture phase when Jesus comes to catch His bride to Heaven and the return stage at least seven years later when the bride of Christ returns to earth with Jesus to rule and reign. This isn't a second and a third coming;

it's one coming in two phases. Jesus is going to come *for* His people, and then He's going to come *with* His people. There's a Rapture, and then there's a return.

Q: Will prodigal children who believed when they were younger but have since stated doubt have an opportunity to change their minds if the Rapture occurs?
A: There will be many people left here on the earth who aren't believers in Christ. Many of those will be people who've heard the gospel before but never really possessed a true faith in Jesus Christ. They will have an opportunity to turn to Christ, repent, and look to Him for salvation, but the Tribulation will be a very difficult experience.

Q: What will those who are left behind think happened at the Rapture?
A: The Bible does not say a lot about how people who are left on earth will respond. However, we do have opinions about what we think will happen. Many will "believe the lie" that is told. We aren't certain what the lie will be, but there could be a wide range of explanations, from UFOs to other kinds of speculations. It will be a great shock when a billion or so people disappear. Shortly thereafter, there is going to be the horrific reality of the Tribulation and judgment that has come upon the earth. According to Revelation 7, there will be a mass revival such as the world has never seen. There will probably be

a mixture of emotions, but shock and fear will be most common.

Q: What happens if you've donated organs to someone and you're raptured? What does that mean for someone who has your donated organ?
A: The state of our pre-raptured body is unimportant related to the Rapture. It doesn't matter if you have donated organs, lost limbs, are dead and cremated, have been lost at sea, or anything else. God will transform what is left of your corrupted, mortal body and give you an immortal, glorious body better than anything you can presently imagine.

If you have donated organs, then hopefully the recipient was also a believer and they will be transformed, and the organ won't matter. But if they are mortal and stay on earth after the Rapture, then the donated organ won't disappear because you won't need it (and they will).

Scripture Index

Notes

1. Defining the Rapture

1. If you research the term *rapture* in English, you will find a variety of spellings for the same term in Latin. There is a reason for that: It is both a verb and a noun, and Latin changes spellings depending on cases for nouns and tenses for verbs. There are also some variations between Latin and Medieval Latin. Scholars generally agree that the word began with Medieval Latin and took its final form in French before it was borrowed in English.

2. Answering Rapture Objections

1. Steve Rudd, "The Origin of Rapture False Doctrine: John Darby 1830 AD," The Interactive Bible, accessed August 27, 2024, https://www.bible.ca/rapture-origin-john-nelson-darby-1830ad.htm.

2. Because of space limitations, we have only touched the surface in regard to historical documents that verify the Rapture has been taught widely and consistently throughout church history. Additional comprehensive resources are available for further research. We recommend Lee W. Brainard and Jeffrey Mardis, *Recent Pre-Trib Findings in the Early Church Fathers* (Harvey, ND: Lee W. Brainard, 2023); Mark Hitchcock and Edward E. Hindson, *Can We Still Believe in the Rapture?* (Eugene: Harvest House Publishers, 2018); and William C. Watson, *Dispensationalism before Darby: Seventeenth-Century and Eighteenth-Century English Apocalypticism* (Silverton, OR: Lampion Press, LLC, 2023).

3. Irenaeus, "Against Heresies, Book V, Chapter 29," trans. Alexander Roberts and William Rambaut, in *Ante-Nicene Fathers*, Vol. 1, ed. Alexander Roberts, James Donaldson, and A. Cleveland Coxe (Buffalo, NY: Christian Literature Publishing Co., 1885), revised and edited for New Advent by Kevin Knight, accessed August 27, 2024, http://www.newadvent.org/fathers/0103529.htm.

4. Lee W. Brainard, "Eusebius—Nine Undiscovered Pretribulation-Rapture Passages," Soothkeep, accessed February 7, 2024, https://soothkeep.info/eusebius-nine-undiscovered-pretribulation-rapture-passages.

5. Ephraem the Syrian, quoted in Thomas D. Ice, "A Brief History of the Rapture," *Article Archives*, 4, May 2009, https://digitalcommons.liberty.edu/pretrib_arch/4.

6. Morgan Edwards, *Two Accidental Exercises on Subjects Bearing the Following Titles: Millennium, Last-Novelties* (Philadelphia: 1788; written in 1744), 7. Available on Pre-Trib Research Center, 2023, https://www.pre-trib.org/articles/rev-morgan-edwards/message/two-academical-exercises-on-subjects-bearing-the-following-titles-millennium-last-novelties/read.

7. Thomas Manton, *A Practical Exposition of the Lord's Prayer* (1684) (Ann Arbor, MI: EEBO Editions, ProQuest, 2010).

8. William Sherwin, *An Antidote Against the Infection of the Times: Or, A Scripture-Prophecy of the Increase of Christ's Kingdom, and the Destruction of Antichrist* (London: Printed for Francis Smith, 1675).

9. *William, Penn, No Cross, No Crown* (London, Printed by Benjamin Clark, 1669).

10. Jonathan Edwards, *A History of the Work of Redemption* (West Linn, OR: Monergism Books, 2010), https://www.monergism.com/thethreshold/sdg/edwards/A%20History%20of%20the%20Work%20of%20Redemp%20-%20Jonathan%20Edwards.pdf.

5. General Signs the Rapture Is Near

1. Fiona Harvey, "World Faces Worst Food Crisis for at Least 50 Years, UN Warns," *The Guardian*, June 9, 2020, https://www.theguardian.com/society/2020/jun/09/world-faces-worst-food-crisis-50-years-un-coronavirus.

2. Open Doors, "World Watch List," accessed August 27, 2024, https://www.opendoors.org/en-US/persecution/countries.